Your Autobiography

Also by Ray Mungo

Your Autobiography

More than 300 Questions to Help You Write Your Personal History

Ray Mungo

MACMILLAN • USA

Macmillan General Reference
A Simon & Schuster Macmillan Company
1633 Broadway
New York, NY 10019

Library of Congress Cataloging-in-Publication Data
Mungo, Raymond, 1946–
    Your autobiography: more than 300 questions to help
you write your personal history/Ray Mungo.–

        p.   cm.
    ISBN 0-02-029545-6
    1. Autobiography—Authorship.   2. Biography as a lit-
erary form.   3. Questions and answers.   I. Title.
CT25.M83   1994
808'.06692–dc20   93–31918   CIP

Macmillan books are available at special discounts for bulk purchases for sales promotions, premiums, fund-raising, or educational use. For details, contact:

Special Sales Director
Macmillan General Reference
A Simon & Schuster Macmillan Company
1633 Broadway
New York, NY 10019
Book Design by Maura Fadden Rosenthal

10   9   8   7   6   5   4   3

Printed in the United States of America

For my mother,
Rita Lafontaine Mungo

Contents

Introduction

Thoughts on Writing Your Autobiography

So you're considering writing your autobiography. Good for you! This means you've given thought to your life and found it has lessons and values that are important to you, things you would like to share with others. You've searched for a higher meaning in the events that have transpired, you seek to dignify the days you've spent here on earth. Your life is too valuable to go unrecorded, forgotten in time.

This book aims to encourage you and guide you through the process of writing your memoirs, which may be a lot easier than you thought. In many years of working with amateur writers who compiled their autobiographies, I have never found an insignificant life, a life without inherent value and great drama. Even if your life story is not intended for a commercial publisher and is not the stuff of gossip columns or heroic achievements, the experiences you have had are your own greatest treasure, well worth the remembering and retelling.

This book is a direct outgrowth of a seminar called "Lit Biz 101," which I founded in Seattle in 1972 and continue to offer in its third decade. The seminar is a beginner's guide to the business of writing and publishing books, and over the years it has attracted hundreds of superb, if amateur, writ-

ers who sought guidance in writing their autobiographies, their memoirs.

Throughout the book, I'll explore specific writing techniques and pose questions for you to
answer, questions that will help you fill in the
details and frame your writing project. This introduction, however, asks you to stand back for a
moment and take a broader, overall look at the
craft of writing autobiography. It's a time-honored
form of writing, one that every great writer has
pursued in one form or another.

Consider these points:

- The essence of good autobiographical writing
  is not in self-praise, but in truthful self-assess-
  ment. Conflict, humility, remorse, and learning from one's mistakes are as much a part of
  good, honest autobiographical writing as tri-
  umph, love, success, or family pride. If your
  book talks about how great and fine your life
  has been on every single page, the average
  reader will find it a crashing bore—and sus-
  pect you're not telling the whole truth. Life's
  greatest heights are achieved through over-
  coming its lows. Your honest autobiography
  will include moments of sadness and struggle
  along with the happy times and major turning
  points.
- Some autobiographies focus on a single, overwhelming accomplishment or event which
  radically changed the author's life. (A good
  example is my friend Dr. Don H. Parker of
  Carmel, California, who was a struggling
  grammar school teacher in Florida until he
  created the SRA Reading Lab system, which
  later was sold to IBM and made him a

wealthy man in his retirement.) If your life turned on a major event, by all means give it the full importance it deserves in your book.

• Nonetheless, autobiography is not necessarily egotistical or self-centered. Many writers are able to add perspective to their story by placing their lives in the wider context of history, ethnic background, family, industry, and friendship. You are the principal character in a drama that unfolds around you, but you are not the root cause of all living, just a player in the mix. Devote plenty of time to describing your loved ones and friends, and show how their lives are entwined with your own.

• The act of writing is a sublime discipline that requires perseverance and determination, but it will repay you many times over. The greatest hurdle to getting the job done is simply finding the time. Have you ever said to yourself: if only I could find the time to sit down and write, my life would make a great book? Welcome to the club. The urge to write a personal or family history is practically universal, but most people just never get around to it. Successful authors are those who diligently put aside time to work on the book, away from life's many distractions. That means a regular, scheduled commitment. The standard here of minimal achievement required at each sitting is easygoing: one sentence is enough! One paragraph is better. One page is a real accomplishment. Look at it this way—if you could write even a page a day, within a year you'd have 365 pages, a pretty hefty book, on your hands! It's not how much you write each time you sit down, it's the patient

· act of adding something, even a word, to your story, and doing it over and over until the thing is done.

(But it's never really the end . . . not while the author is alive, anyway.)

• Your life is your stock in trade, your unique history, a book that you alone could write. No historian of the future could ever retrace the events of your life with half the realism that you can provide. Even if you think your life has been obscure or unimportant to the world, it's important to you—and that's what counts. If one reader, perhaps a child or grandchild, personal friend, or even a stranger, gains some wisdom or knowledge or humor from reading what you've written, you have shared your life in a way that only you are capable of doing. If our existence on this planet has any meaning at all, your life is part of it. Don't sell yourself short. Your book matters.

• There is a profound continuity in the family of letters, which you contribute to when you write your memoirs. Just by writing, you are doing your part to keep up civilization. I can't say this too strongly. Nowadays, we tend to videotape major events like marriage, childbirth, vacations, and even funerals. Nothing wrong with that, but reading and writing puts you in the realm of education and creativity in a way that videotape will never do. If literacy fails, the whole standard of civilized culture goes with it. By adding your voice to the body of written work, you can achieve a kind of immortality, or at least a kinship with the Muse.

- Writing your life story helps you understand your own life, to better comprehend the forces that changed and defined you, through examination and analysis. In hindsight, the considered life lets you observe patterns of behavior, lessons learned the hard way, mistakes you didn't make twice, pleasures made even better by reliving them in memory.
- The best writing is simple, straightforward. You don't have to squelch the poet in you, who might lean toward a little prose embellishment; but when you're telling a story, the best way to do it is simply, letting us know what happened. Put words together that the reader can quickly grasp. Write as if you were speaking, telling a yarn. Don't repeat yourself or drag out the punch line of a joke. Make one thought lead to the next. Don't be afraid to edit, cross out, rewrite, and distill your prose until you get the perfect "spin" on your story. I recommend Strunk and White's classic book *The Elements of Style*, a timeless primer in the art of good writing. Even professional writers should go back and read it again every few years.
- Seek the help of others. The best writers benefit from the work of their editors, after all. If you have a friend or relative with writing expertise who's willing to critique or review your work, take advantage of it. Another great help is attending writers' workshops and seminars where you can meet other memoirists and compare each other's stories. Your writing skill can really grow under the care and nurturing of readers, friends, workshop leaders, etc. Writing needn't be a lonely endeavor,

although it's normal at first to be a bit embarrassed when having your work reviewed or read by others, since you're not used to it.

• Reading and writing go together. If you want to learn how to write well, read the work of those who do. Read others' memoirs, the published ones you find in bookstores and libraries, and the unpublished variety you find in workshops and writers' conferences. Especially read the memoirs of those whose lives have something in common with your own.

• Follow an outline. It's fine to digress or get distracted, but don't throw a hodgepodge of unrelated stories together. Form your outline, or plan, in advance and stick to it. One easy system is to create chapter titles, and write a few sentences describing the chapter contents. This organization makes your writing task much easier. All you have to do is follow the plan you've created.

You can easily see the outline I followed in writing this book, and you can use the chapter titles from this book as guidelines, changing them from the second person "you" form to the first person "I" form, and from the question format to the declaratory. Your chapter headings would be "Where I Came From," "How I Came of Age," "Life Began at Forty," and so forth. Or you can devise your own chapter headings and scheme.

• Put your experience into the context of lessons. Life is like school, you learn new lessons every day. Your writing should show what you learned from experience. "My mother's love taught me to be kind." "My business failure taught me to never again trust a partner to handle the money." "After watching the dignity with which my wife handled her cancer and hospitalization, I realized she had taught me how to die, with spirit intact."

- Visualize as you write. Form your written words into a kind of picture. Close your eyes (if that helps) and imagine a scene out of your past, actually bring up a mental image. Listen to what the characters say. Smell the aromas, hear the noises from that remembered scene. Now, write the scene as a moving photographic image you are presenting to the reader. If you can visualize and remember details, you can write the story! Just report on what you see.

For example: "The winter nights were cold and dark in Michigan. My father sat by the oil burner stove in the kitchen in his favorite chair, reading the afternoon paper and fiddling with his pipe. My mother peeled potatoes and walloped her meat loaf in a blue ceramic bowl. Liberace came on TV and my grandmother rushed to put on her earrings, pearls, and good dress. She was quite old when TV came into being, and she believed Liberace could actually see her as well as she could see him, so she wanted to look nice for him."

- Write as if your life depended on it. Your life may not change one iota whether you write it down or not, but other people reading your work will judge your life based on how well you've told the story. Enhance the dignity, charm, and meaning of your life by taking the time and effort to write it carefully.
- Don't waste time worrying about whether you can do this. Just go ahead and try, and the chances are overwhelmingly in your favor. If you can write a letter to a friend or relative, if

you write notes in greeting cards, if you leave written messages for family members on the kitchen table—in short, if you do the most basic, simple kinds of writing—then you can write the story of your life. Keep it simple, and keep at it, and you'll succeed.

Now, let's get started with some easy "questions that define you."

Your Autobiography

WHO ARE YOU?

The question of who you are is determined by your experience, because life creates and shapes us out of whatever raw talents and resources we are born with. Your life is a series of answers, which can be lengthy and detailed, to fundamental questions about what happened to you. No matter how "ordinary" your life may seem, each of us has stories and feelings of great passion, love, death, cataclysmic events in our private memory vaults—stories worth keeping and sharing.

This book is a series of questions, questions that define you. By answering them honestly in your own words, you can tell a great story that you alone are qualified to tell—the story of your life. It doesn't have to be glamorous, you don't need to be rich or famous or have climbed Mount Everest. Your life is your own, the stuff of legend, the stuff of literature.

You are the subject of this book, as well as your own book. You are the whole reason it exists, and your life is the plot.

The instinct to tell your own story is a basic, primal human drive. It's natural to want to remember and pass along the experiences that have shaped your life, the many changes and triumphs and pitfalls you have known. You want to preserve these stories (and photos and information) so they won't be lost to future generations. Once you die, this book ends. While you're alive and remembering, please tell us your story!

All you have to do to write your autobiography is sit down and answer the questions in this book as honestly as you can, fleshing out the details, filling in the story in your own words. Your writing style doesn't have to match that of Hemingway, and you don't need to worry unduly about correct spelling and grammar unless you also aim to have the story published commercially. The main thing is you want to stimulate your memory, re-create the moments of greatest significance in your life, paint a verbal picture of what it was like.

You don't need a commercial publisher to benefit from the rewarding process of collecting your memoirs. In the very act of writing about your life, you examine and understand it better and see yourself in the big picture. It is a rewarding experience. You can, of course, also publish the autobiography yourself in limited editions reproduced economically for family and friends.

Many people who want to write their memoirs fear they lack the ability to write a book. It's a daunting task, to be sure, but in this volume our simple question and answer format allows you to jog your memory, research your past, record your great accomplishments and important moments of your life, and gradually build that book of your own. You may want to dictate stories onto audio tape, but be advised that it takes a great deal of time and work to transcribe those tapes into a manuscript. You may find it easier than you think to sit down and compose the stories at a typewriter or word processor, or by hand.

The questions will define you through all stages of your life, starting with before you were even born, with memories of your parents and grandparents, stories they may have told you about their lives. In that way, and because you'll include your children and grandchildren as well, your own life story actually encompasses multiple generations.

Your family isn't the whole of your life, naturally. You need to also include your experiences at work, your friendships, and larger events in the world which influenced your fate. Today's seniors have seen in a single lifetime profound changes that rival the greatest developments in history. Seventy-five years ago, the world was a quieter place. But you remained yourself through all the turmoil, a single person adjusting to the ever-changing environment around you.

Examine who you are in terms of these four categories of experience: physical, emotional, professional, and philosophical. All four will be discussed again in greater length with many specific questions for you to answer. But take the time now, as you begin the adventure of writing your life story, to see the larger scope of your life.

Physical

The body you inhabited at birth is the cornerstone of your existence, although physical realities are not everything in life, and for some people not even the most important thing. We've all heard

stories of courageous people who overcame physical obstacles like handicaps, birth defects, life-
threatening surgery or grave illness, to go on to a
good life worth living. Just about any physical dis-
ability can be overcome or at least tolerated.

Your physical reality begins at birth, a flesh and
bone manifestation of the life given to you by your
parents. Many physical aspects are set in stone,
things you can't easily change. For starters, there's
gender, and although women are finally gaining
equality, you had a different life in this country if
you were born female rather than male any time
before the 1960s. It was a "man's world" most of
that time, and change has come slowly. (Nor
should anyone think that a "woman's work" is any
less important and dignified than a man's. What,
indeed, could be more important work than the
raising of children, shaping of their minds and
lives, a task largely given to women in our culture?)

Of course, in this day and age most physical
traits can be altered, even including gender.
Although such cases are rare, they have led to
some outstanding autobiography indeed. The
great travel writer Jan Morris wrote *Conundrum,* a
book in which she explains how she changed from
being James Morris, faithful husband and father.

Race is important in a society that has practiced
virulent racism for hundreds of years and contin-
ues to so do despite some progress. If you were
born black in America, you had two strikes against
your economic and educational prospects, what
with segregation and Jim Crow laws. While conditions improved for middle class blacks, the great
shame of the nation is that we have yet to eliminate
discrimination. Hispanics, Asians, indeed every
minority racial group, have been oppressed.

Your parents and their genes write a bioprescription for your physical presence. That's why researching your family history is so interesting. You inherit all manner of genetic traits from both of your parents. You'll never be more or less than the sum product of your parents' genes commingling, so the more you can remember about their bodies, the pattern of their illnesses, and the physical lives of their parents—your grandparents—the more you'll learn about yourself.

Your sexual orientation may be determined genetically before birth, if recent studies are accurate. Research by Dr. Simon Levay at the University of California, San Diego, suggests that the heterosexual majority has a different brain shape from the homosexual minority. These studies are controversial, but people do tend to exhibit their sex drive and orientation at an early age. Your height, weight, lifestyle, money (or lack of it), and health for better or worse are all crucial factors in your physical well-being, your bodily reality.

Emotional

Your emotional life can be even more important than anything about your physical situation. If you've been blessed with loving parents, a good marriage, children who love you, and friends who care, you have had a wonderful life regardless of how many struggles, problems, or even catastrophes you've had to endure.

Parents pass along to their children an inherent sense of self-worth based on feelings of love and affection. Experts say these good feelings are crucial to a child's emotional development, that an infant or young child absorbs love as a real nutrient. Even if one of your parents died or was taken away from you at an early age, you may have a kind of vague but real memory of that person from earliest infancy, perhaps from when you were still in the womb.

After the great love and emotional foundation that only a parent (natural or adoptive) can provide comes the love of your brothers and sisters, your partners in life because they are the only people who share your genetic background (if they are children of the same two parents, that is). Siblings usually fight and compete for their parents' attention, but later in life you may find that nobody knows you and loves you more than a brother or sister, especially after your parents have died.

Your children are an extension of your heart as well as your body, so even if they are adopted or stepchildren, they will form a major part of your emotional self. Notice how devoted typical parents are to their kids, to the point of making real sacrifices in their own lives. You too may have lived a large part of your life mostly for the kids' sake.

Friends are very important to your emotional health, and friendship is something that each of us treasures beyond price. Put another way, if you don't have friends more valuable to you than money, you're very poor. No matter how close you may be to your family, friends are still an invaluable part of your emotional life. The love between good and old friends is the reward for giving of yourself freely.

Finally, but in truth most important, is the love you share with your spouse or mate or lover, your "significant other" person, or in some cases with more than one person you have married or loved. Although many people are single by choice, there is an abiding value in marriage and mating that

affects everyone. We all yearn for the perfect coun-
terpart, the other half, and if you have enjoyed that
kind of companionship, you can only be grateful.

Professional

The work life you have had may be extremely
close to your heart, coming right after the physical
and emotional things and perhaps even dominat-
ing your waking thoughts more than family or
friendships ever did. For some of us, professional
accomplishments are the greatest satisfaction in
being alive.

Consider what work you've done to earn your
bread and roof, what you did with your time.
Looking at your professional life as a whole,
remember and write down the stages of your
advancement. First, you may have learned or
apprenticed in your business with someone else,
perhaps a teacher in college or the employer who
gave you your first job opportunity. As you grew
more proficient at your trade, opportunities came
up, changes occurred, promotions were given.
Entrepreneurs and the self-employed very often
have interesting and adventuresome work histories, too.

If you worked for the same company for a long
time, chances are you interacted with a large cast
of fellow employees, friends, clients, competitors.
It's possible the workplace became a second home
to you. You may have even preferred the office or
shop to your real home if you are the workaholic
type or had domestic problems. My father spent
over thirty years at the same paper manufacturing
company in Lawrence, Massachusetts, and he sim-

ply loved the place. He was editor of the company magazine, a chronicler of the lives and generations of his co-workers. Every night over supper, we listened to Dad's litany of what happened to Charlie and Vinny and Joe, the guys on his shift, that day. Sometimes on weekends too, he cheerfully went to work, taking us kids along so we could play on the electric adding machines and typewriters, run around the abandoned factory equipment, and slurp nickel Cokes from the vending machine. Forced into retirement in his middle sixties, my father was miserable without his job, and he lived only two years after leaving Merrimack Paper.

If the work you did in your life is something you are proud of, your book is the place to record it, honor it, describe and relive it, and save it for posterity.

Philosophical

In youth, a kind of idealism or naïveté may have inspired you to love, work, travel, or study. As experience grows, that youthful ardor can be tempered by setbacks and disillusionments, but you're a lucky person if you can filter through the bad and harvest the good things in life. You discover in your philosophy of life which values have really endured.

Defining a philosophy of life is one of the most difficult things a person can do, but as you get older you naturally ruminate on what in your life was most worthwhile. For many of us, it's family, religion, social service, love of country, some combination of those values. For some people, it's art or literature or political ideology, freedom and peace. You can define your own philosophy through key words, common experiences that may be particularly enlightening, the *highlights* of your life. Put simply: what are the principles dearest to your heart? What do you believe in? What guiding ideals made your life worth living? What did you learn from living?

Your philosophy of life is important not only to yourself but to your children, grandchildren, anyone who may happen to read your memoirs. Don't be shy about telling them what you've learned, and don't leave out the hard parts or the difficult lessons. So, to begin, ask yourself the question, "Who am I?" and answer it with a broader view than merely stating your name or place of birth. This exercise leads into Chapter 2, "Whom Do You Come From?" in which you will record memories of your parents and details of your background. But the question of who you are encompasses a gestalt, a perceived selfhood that is more than the sum of its parts.

Don't be discouraged if you don't have an answer for every one of these questions, and don't limit the length of your answers. Write freely, everything that comes to mind. Even professional writers will tell you the important thing is getting the words on the paper—they can be edited, shortened, corrected, or rewritten later, but you have to have something to work with.

Now consider:

What was your given name at birth?

Who gave you that name? Was there any particular reason, such as being named after a grandparent, parent, saint, or one of your parents' friends or heroes?

What's your name today, if different from your birth name, and how did it change—through marriage, adoption, legal name change?

Are you married, single, divorced, widowed? Who is your spouse or partner or, if he or she is deceased, who were they?

How old are you? When and where were you born?

What do you, or did you, do for a living? How do you see yourself professionally?

Does your work define your identity, or do you see yourself more in terms of family role or personal interests? In other words, if your name is Jim and you're a plumber, do you see yourself as "Jim the Plumber" or rather "Jim the man, husband of Joanne, father of Jeff, Red Sox fan, avid skier, who happens to make a living as a plumber"?

Where do you live, and why?

Do you belong to a religion? Political party or affiliation? Membership group or association? Do you define yourself by these affiliations (for example, "I'm a Republican Methodist from Tennessee and a proud member of the Kiwanis Club and American Legion") or would you describe yourself as independent, even a maverick?

Do you have children or grandchildren? List their names and dates of birth.

How is your health? If you have problems, what are they and what is the prognosis for improvement?

Are you financially secure? If so, what's your greatest asset, the thing that is the cornerstone of your stability? A home that you own, a generous pension, a portfolio? If not, what would you need to achieve security now?

What do you really like to do? If money and health were no problem, and you could choose any activity that pleases you, how would you spend your time?

Who are your friends? Who would you most enjoy being with? (Your spouse may also be your best friend, of course.)

Do you have brothers or sisters? How many, what ages? Most important, how much older or younger than you are they?

How did your siblings' lives turn out? How did they differ from yours, and why?

Would your parents be proud of what you have accomplished in your lifetime? Does your experience amount to a better life than your parents had, or not?

If you died right now, what would you want on your tombstone? Write your own epitaph, a pithy statement on your life.(Sample answers to the above question from a group of writers included: "Be right back." "He never blew a deadline." "She stuck to good cheer through thick and thin.")

If you could leave some great gift or discovery, some true help to mankind, what would it be?

Granted, some of these questions cannot be answered in a few simple words. Some of them invite a whole essay. But they all relate to the question of your perceived identity, who you are, what influences made you yourself, and what kind of message and story you can write for your own enjoyment and the edification of your readers.

Just tell it like it is. Be honest when you answer these questions, and don't worry about who is going to read it eventually or about offending anyone. Your autobiography is your turn, your version of events, your view of things. In telling the truth as you see it, you may confront some painful realizations and difficult paragraphs, but no memoir is written and no life lived without struggle and work.

"Although nobody's life makes any sense, if you're going to make a book out of it you might as well make it into a story," wrote journalist Russell Baker in his memoir, *Life with Mother*. After his mother's death, Baker found her marriage certificate in an old trunk. "And I looked at it: she was married in March of the year in which I was born in August," Baker wrote. "I was fifty-four years old and I realized I was a love child."

Everybody's got stories like that, funny and sad and human. Now you're ready. Let's take a ride through your life, see a movie of your experience, write a book of your memoirs. It's easier than you think, it's enjoyable and invaluable. Turn to the next chapter, "Whom Do You Come From?" and begin to piece this priceless story together.

WHOM DO YOU COME FROM?

"You don't realize it, being American, but you come from a great line of Samurai," wrote Auntie Aiko in Kamakura, Japan, to her nephew Richard Yamamoto in Los Angeles, a third-generation Japanese-American who knows more about Hollywood than Tokyo's Ginza. Born in California, he "comes from" there, but nonetheless he derives from the ancestors who preceded him. He's a Samurai, too.

Each of us comes from our parents, their parents, and so forth, back into genealogical history, as well as from some particular city or country. We are the products of the people who bore and raised us, our tribes, nations, and ethnic enclaves.

Even if you were adopted as a child and have no personal memory of your birth parents or grandparents, you can't change who you came from, can't alter that genetic makeup you inherited. Adopted people, in fact, are more likely than others to develop a keen interest in tracing their roots. When denied physical evidence of their natural parents, they often hunger for information about their progenitors because it holds the key to their own identities.

Most of us, of course, knew our parents and grandparents, aunts and uncles, maybe even great-grandparents, and heard stories of the past told by older relatives. By piecing together what you have heard, then adding research and speculation, you might be able to create a highly accurate picture of the people you "came from," and what their lives were like.

That's important because in writing the story of your life, you will quickly discover that it's intertwined inextricably with the lives of your predecessors. Not that your fate was utterly predetermined by your background—many folks achieve success despite coming from a poor or disadvantaged background, and so have a better story to tell. But your essence will always be the sum of your genetic parts, passed on to you by the people who made you.

Begin this exercise and chapter by answering a simple series of questions that define your "people power."

How far back can you trace your ancestry? Do you know the names, dates of birth, geographical homes, or other information about your grandparents, great-grandparents, great-great-grandparents, and so forth? Where does the trail begin, who is the oldest ancestor you can name?

Your parents, grandparents, etc.—who were they? Where were they born, and how did they come to live where they did? Make a list of names, dates, places, details.

Who was the oldest relative you had personal experience of? Remember and write down an incident, anything at all, that happened between you and that oldest relative. I remember, for example, being sent to the corner grocery with my aged French-Canadian grandmother, who spoke no English, to act as her interpreter. But when she was given an overripe tomato, she loudly protested to the shopkeeper in passable English. Then, on the way home, she made me promise not to tell. I was seven, she was seventy-seven, but we were like two kids playing hooky together.

What was your mother like? Where was she born, what was her birth name, how many brothers and sisters did she have, and what were their names? Did she ever talk about growing up, and what it was like for her? Write a brief story about something that happened in your mother's childhood, as told to you by her.

And your father, same questions. What forces shaped his destiny, and how did they affect his life? What did he do for a living, and how did he feel about it? Who were his parents, his siblings and his friends?

(These could be long lists, of course. My mother was one of twenty children, my father one of thirteen. I had aunts and uncles by the score, and cousins by the dozens.)

Meditate on your parents for a while. How did they meet? Whatever brought them together also, in an extended sense, brought life to you. Whom do you have to thank, what lucky stars crossed in the heavens?

Did your parents get along? (Were those stars indeed lucky for them?) Did they really love each other, merely tolerate being married, or actively dislike each other? There can be a good deal of pain in confronting questions like these, questions that define your own attitude toward marriage and partnership perhaps, but the truth is worth any risk of anguish.

How did your parents feel about their own parents? That simple question may help illuminate how you feel toward your mother and father. If one of your parents was abused or abandoned as a child, you may have grown up hearing bitter stories or outright renunciations. Even if your grandfather was an industrial tycoon held in high regard by the world, he may have been a monster to his own children. On the other hand, if your parents retained strong feelings of love and loyalty toward their parents, you are more likely to feel the same way toward them.

If every little quirk and neurotic tendency disqualified people from being parents, most of us would never have been born. Ask yourself, then, what funny or strange habits your parents had. Maybe your father hated cucumbers (mine did) but absolutely adored ice cream. Maybe your mother never got over some real or imagined slight a third-grade teacher perpetrated on her, and developed a lifelong distrust of teachers and schools.

Did your father or mother ever do something that embarrassed you with your school friends? Were you ever ashamed to bring friends into your home for fear of some erratic behavior by your parents? Did you ever suffer humiliation at the hands of your peers because your parents were old-fashioned, different, poor, unsophisticated, drunk, snobby, hypercritical, unfriendly, *too* friendly, or some other wrong and horrible thing to a child's mind?

Did your parents ever give you a special gift for your birthday or holiday, a gift that remains in your mind as something wonderful and unforgettable? Write it down, describe it. (In my case, it was a red bicycle with a checkered seat. I was twelve; we couldn't afford it, but my father paid for it in time payments from his thirty-five-dollar-a-week job.)

Did you have a favorite aunt or uncle, grandparent, or other older relative (aside from your parents) who took a special interest in you, gave you gifts, took you on outings to pleasant destinations? Describe that person and the attention you received.

Let the memories, painful and happy and sad and lovely, all wash over you, reminding you of whom you came from and how those people shaped your life.

What values did your parents and guardians instill in you? What were you taught was right and wrong? Indeed, what values of your parents did you *reject* in your own life? These may be the most important questions of all. Good parents always try to pass along to their children some general framework of values in life. It's a natural instinct, not even necessarily preconsidered. Children, in turn, delight in flaunting the old folks' philosophy, but the influence remains. Did you ever notice how, as you got older, you started resembling your parents more and more, even repeating the same phrases they said, teaching your own children the same lessons your parents taught you and you initially rejected?

When writing about your ancestors, consider the study of genealogy, the science of researching your roots. Not remarkably, humanity has long practiced the business of recording lives. Birth, marriage, and death records exist in all but the most primitive societies, as people everywhere recognize the value in keeping written documentation of our existence. These records are our history, the evidence which dignifies our existence and proves its importance.

You might find yourself surprised at how much you can learn about your relatives if you try. If you can simply identify the town or city where a grandparent was born, for example, you might find birth and family records kept in that town which lead you to more information going further back in time. Cemeteries and old headstones contain valuable data, city and county governments keep old records indefinitely, libraries and private genealogers maintain vast stores of information, facts that may be of little interest to anyone else but which could help define you!

Medical science knows the value of family history. That's why doctors often ask you to fill out a questionnaire describing the incidence of certain diseases and common illnesses in your family. Afflictions like diabetes, heart murmurs, vision problems, tuberculosis, and mental illness are definitely known to "run in the family."

We all have two families (or more!) of course—our mother's and our father's—and each of those families also had two sides, and so on, back into history until we are "coming from" millions of disparate entities.

For Isidore Myers, seventy-five, a retired real estate management executive of Newport Beach, California, research into his roots and family history became an obsession and, finally, a kind of sacred mission. His Polish family had been almost entirely wiped out by the Nazis during World War II. Only one relative survived the Holocaust, while one hundred and fifteen others were killed.

In 1989, Myers made a trip to the small town of Wlodawa, on the Polish-Russian border, and visited the Sobibor extermination camp, where he saw a large tomb filled with ashes and human bones that stirred him to a total commitment to writing the story of his family. He spent three years and $50,000 tracing every old photograph, letter, and family reminiscence he could find to create a handsome 279-page book called "Remember: A Book to Honor the Family I Never Knew."

He described the labor as "like gathering a bunch of threads and making a quilt out of it." He made hundreds of phone calls, wrote many letters, spent countless hours in libraries. Every clue, every tiny scrap of information, led to another. In 1992, he self-published a thousand copies of the book, donating many of them to libraries and Holocaust centers worldwide. Although he's enjoyed great success in business and a fine family with his wife Penny and two sons, Myers feels that his book is his proudest accomplishment.

"By gaining knowledge of our roots and paying tribute to the memory of our kin who were

Holocaust victims, we rob Hitler of his ultimate victory—the loss of their memories," Myers wrote in the book.

Janine M. of Brookline, Massachusetts, converted by marriage to the Church of Latter Day Saints (Mormon), a religion which places great emphasis on genealogy, and uncovered startling evidence about the paternal grandfather she had never met. Growing up in the 1950s and 1960s, she had been told that her grandfather was dead. He was seldom discussed in the home, and no photo or other remembrance of him was ever seen. But after her father died in 1985 and Janine began researching through his papers, she discovered that *his* father had spent the last twenty-five years of his life locked up in a state-run insane asylum at Manchester, New Hampshire, and in fact the old man was very much alive during Janine's childhood, and only fifty miles away.

Clearly, the family must have had reasons to wish the grandfather dead, or at least permanently absent. Nobody ever visited him in the hospital, records showed. When she managed to get the entire hospital file on her grandfather, Janine learned even more. Her own father and his mother had signed the commitment papers, and her grandfather was not so much "crazy" as extremely depressed. The detailed records of her grandfather's mental condition were immensely valuable to Janine, who herself had suffered episodes of clinical depression during an unhappy first marriage. Her brother Roger had also had bouts of severe depression and he too learned a lot from the medical records of their lately discovered grandparent.

"If we knew then what we know now, my grandfather could have been rescued," Janine said. "His condition was never bad enough to warrant involuntary commitment for twenty-five years, but back in the 1940s anybody could be locked up if two family members signed the papers. The laws of New Hampshire wouldn't tolerate that now."

At the top of the chapter, I mentioned the letter Richard Yamamoto got from his aunt in Kamakura, Japan, telling him he was a Samurai despite being a third-generation American. After getting the letter, Richard took a long-dreamed-of trip to Japan, a nation that his own parents had never visited. Richard's life had been about as non-Japanese as possible. His family lived in a part of L.A. better known for its Jewish population than Asian immigrants. Richard and his brothers were the sole Asian-American kids in Fairfax High School. At thirteen, he'd complained to his mother that he wanted a Bar Mitzvah, since all his school friends were having one.

But at twenty-five, Richard found himself thrust into the strange world of Japan, a country in which he looked perfectly normal but couldn't speak the language or read the street signs. "People reacted to me as if I was retarded," he said. "I had a Japanese face, but the minute I opened my mouth they knew something was wrong. I didn't get the same understanding and courtesy that a white foreigner would have. People just thought I was stupid or something."

Fortunately, Auntie Aiko spoke perfect English, having spent her life married to a career diplomat who held ambassadorial posts around the world. She regaled Richard with stories and photos of his famous Samurai forebears. She even gave him a seventeenth-century sword of priceless value, a family heirloom, and asked him if he'd like to take over managing the family estate, which had fallen into disrepair since her husband's death. The house and grounds overlooked Kamakura Bay, a true ancestral mansion.

Richard sensed in all this the potential for sudden wealth and land holdings, but his heart remained in Hollywood and he doubted he could be happy in Kamakura. He did, however, learn so much about his Samurai heritage that he returned to California and took up the study of Japanese history and culture, eventually earning a master's degree from the Monterey Institute of International Studies. He credits his aunt with kindling his interest in these studies.

"I'm more of a complete person now that I understand the people I came from and how their lives affected mine," he said at age thirty-seven. "There's no substitute for the value of knowing your personal evolution."

If you want to define yourself, to find out who you are, to write your life story, there's no better place to start than with your progenitors. They are where you are truly "coming from." They are the first chapter in your history, even before your own birth—which follows in our next chapter, "Where Were You Born?"

3

WHERE WERE YOU BORN (AND WHAT WAS IT LIKE)?

"I was born in a howling blizzard in February 1946, in one of those awful mill towns in eastern Massachusetts, and lived to tell about it." That was the first sentence of my first book, *Famous Long Ago,* an autobiographical coming-of-age tale set in the 1960s. The "awful mill town" remains awful. As for my birth, I can only admit that the town and its circumstances certainly shaped me.

Where were *you* born? What was it like?

The second question seems to be a joke, because of course we don't "remember" what it was like to be born, but the meaning is simply "what circumstances surrounded your birth?" Your birth is of consummate importance to your autobiography, of course. It is the true beginning of your life story, notwithstanding the importance of your parents and other ancestors. We tend to measure our success in life by what we've accomplished in relation to our birth expectations. The child of a rich tycoon might well be expected to manage an empire, for example, but when the ragman's son achieves fame and fortune, that's news.

There is a popular weakness for rags to riches stories. President Bill Clinton in his 1992 campaign

made a point of his humble birth to a widowed
mother, in a small house in Hope, Arkansas. The
image was touching: a President born in Hope,
offering hope to the beleaguered American people,
himself an example of how one's disadvantages at
birth can be turned into worldly success.

Maybe that's why I chose to mention the "awful
mill town" and "howling blizzard" as primary factors in my birth, to suggest that I'd survived
adverse circumstances. That approach stirs sympathy in the average reader. But we're all avidly
interested in the lives of the rich and powerful as
well, so if you were born in the lap of power and
luxury, that's fascinating too. Most of us, of course,
were neither paupers nor royalty when born, but
somewhere in the vast middle class.

So, tell us about your birth. Reconstruct this
momentous event as best you can based on what
you know or have heard from relatives.

What was the month, day, and year and what time
of day or night were you born? The time of birth is
crucial to construction of an astrological chart,
since it determines your rising or ascendant sign of
the zodiac. But even if you don't believe in horo-
scopes, the question is interesting. Some birth certificates indicate the time of birth but many do not,
and you'll have to rely on what your mother or
some other close relative remembers.

What can you tell us about the place where you
were born? Was it a prosperous center for manufacturing, a sophisticated major city, a rural back-
water? How many people lived in the town? What
kind of housing did your parents have? What was
their address?

How many, if any, brothers and sisters preceded you into life? How old were they when you were born? How many siblings were born after you arrived? Who else lived in the household? Were any of your grandparents, aunts, or uncles living at home or nearby?

What was your given name, and why were you given that name? Are you a junior or a third? Other than your legal name, were you called by a nickname or diminutive and did you like or hate the nickname? Did you ever rename yourself or insist on being called something other than your "real" name?

Were you born into a particular religion, baptized perhaps? What is your racial background, and your parents' races? How much did you weigh, what color were your hair and eyes?

Close your eyes for a moment and consider the state of the world on the day you were born. Things were certainly different then. Your mother may have done her laundry by hand or with a wringer washer, hanging the clothes outdoors to dry on a line. Your father might have driven a horse-drawn buggy or trudged to work through the snow. Perhaps they lived in a faraway country whose borders no longer exist.

What kind of weather typified the place you were born? Were you born somewhere with a harsh winter climate like Poland or Maine (or even Poland, Maine), or in the steamy tropics of Florida? Were you born in an August heat wave, an April shower?

Author Stephen Diamond, who wrote the novel *Panama Red*, was born in Miami Beach and grew up in Panama City with journalist parents who published an international tourism magazine. After years of working in New York and New England, he finally settled in Santa Barbara, California, because the early experience of balmy winters and torrid summers had left him unwilling to permanently tolerate snow and ice. My father, on the other hand, was such a New Englander that he considered an L.A. Christmas without snow as practically immoral.

What was the geography of your birthplace like? Your temperament and lifestyle are dramatically affected by the kind of landscape you hail from. It's said the wind-blown, open desert creates singular, lonesome, independent people, while city dwellers tend to be more socially adjusted. Germans are intellectually severe, French people earthy, Italians romantic. These are clichés, of course, but not without some basis in reality. The physical place you are born dictates an enormous part of your future life. It's almost always luckier to be born in the United States than in Haiti, for example. If you were born on a farm or ranch (and stayed through childhood), you had a greatly different start from someone born in Detroit. In birth, as in real estate, "location is everything."

What happened in the nation and world the year you were born? Who was President or King or Queen, what major social forces were at work? Great events shape the lives of ordinary people. The reason the baby boomers began arriving in 1946 was the return of U.S. troops from World

War II. Born in 1929, you were a Depression baby. "Notch babies" are Social Security recipients born in an early twentieth-century span of years that doomed them to a lower benefit payment. The year of your birth says a lot about your life.

I'm barely old enough to remember the iceman and the milkman. My family didn't acquire a TV until I was six or seven and had already learned to read, beginning a lifelong passion for the printed word. I remember a quaint, sometimes harsh world in which we didn't have modern conveniences, but childhood memories are fond. The first President I can remember is Eisenhower, first movie *Bambi*, first musical record *Annie Get Your Gun*.

How comfortable were your parents when you were born? Were you born into wealth, poverty, or somewhere in between? Describe your family's financial situation, how they survived (if they did), and the house or apartment your parents had on the day of your birth.

If you happened to grow up in the house you were born into, indulge yourself in a comprehensive memory of its features. What did it look like, smell like? Did it have cubbyholes, attic, cellar, barn, rooftop, closets, or hidden areas you played in as a child? Did you have a secret garden or a clubhouse where grownups were barred?

If you grew up someplace other than where you were born, you can still reconstruct the site of your beginning with the help of memory, both your own and relatives' rememberings, plus photos, published history, and research through family records.

If your birthplace itself has a fascinating history, don't hesitate to write it. I might have done better with that "awful mill town" by simply admitting it was Lawrence, Massachusetts, site of historically famous workers' strikes and cradle of the American labor movement, as well as of luminaries like poet Robert Frost and composer Leonard Bernstein.

The place you were born says a lot about you. Don't hesitate to say a lot about it in your autobiography!

Jane La B. wrote in her first "Lit Biz 101" class:

> I now realize that I already understood military terminology on the day I was born. My parents were both professional Army officers, and we moved every few years throughout my childhood, living on bases all over Germany and the Philippines and the U.S. My older brothers were all trained little cadets, raised by a father who treated them as recruits, and when they finally had a daughter, my folks couldn't conceive of a different upbringing, so I became one of the boys. But I marched to a different drummer. I hid lipstick in my school uniform pocket.

Steve S. had a different beginning:

> People think it must be a privilege to be born the grandson of a leading national politician (a U.S. senator), of a family with a famous name and rich history. And I'm not denying the advantages that name has brought me. But it was also a curse.
> Because I was a male heir to the family, with its financial and political importance, many things were expected of me that no ordinary child would have to worry about. From earliest childhood, I was

taught that we were different, we were "leaders" and expected to excel in every way. The pressure was on before I started kindergarten.

It was as if I had enrolled in Harvard at birth, which wasn't far from literally true. My father and grandfather, both Harvard men, announced my birth in the alumni magazine, and I was christened in a Harvard football jersey!

Mari J. had an interesting start in life:

I was born on a Chinese junk bobbing in the harbor at Penang, Malaysia, where my mother and father were missionaries attempting to convert the half Chinese, half Malay population to Christianity. The predominant religion in the country was Muslim. The year was 1925. My folks had run out of money and were taken in by the charity of a Christian Chinese family who fished for a living. Although my given name was Mari, our host family called me Little Fish, because I was born under the sign of Pisces, the fishes.

To pay for the midwife and baby clothes, my father sold a gold watch his father had given him when my parents left Cleveland on their sacred mission. He got 800 Malay dollars for the watch, enough in those times to live for several months on rice and steamed vegetables twice a day, plus rudimentary medical care for the baby and a rent donation for the watery accommodations.

I never would have known about the watch except that my father got it back when I was about ten. We were in Hong Kong by then, Dad had been promoted to the head of the ministry, and he found the watch at a pawn shop, clearly inscribed with my grandfather's name. It was the only time I ever saw him cry.

I felt guilty that he was forced to sell the watch because of my birth. "Princess," he said, "nothing in the world made me happier than seeing you born." Getting his father's watch back, however, was something pretty wonderful.

Now that you've answered many questions about the place you were born, try to see the "big picture" of your life in terms of where you came from. Consider how the place affected your life. Whether you wandered far and wide or stayed in the same place your whole life, your hometown will always be just that: a place where your great life story began.

4

DID YOU HAVE A HAPPY CHILDHOOD?

"You're never too old to have a happy childhood," novelist Tom Robbins wrote. The line was so appealing that See's, a chain of candy and chocolate stores in the West, used it in its advertising until Robbins's attorney forced them to desist. But in terms of your autobiography, the simple question of whether you had a happy childhood can move you to tears regardless of the response, because your childhood influenced your entire life.

Did you have a happy childhood, and if so, why; if not, why not? Contrary to an adult's point of view, children's happiness usually doesn't depend on material wealth. As long as they have their basic needs met, lots of love, and a stimulating environment that provides them fun in growing and learning, kids are happy. We're speaking of young children, of course, not teenagers who may need cars and condoms and nights at the prom.

Most people come to a compromise on this question, reasoning that their childhood was as happy as it could have been under the circumstances, but nonetheless these questions can evoke very painful memories indeed.

In answering questions about your childhood,

you are reinventing yourself through your emotional development. Many writers can unlock a door to profound self-realization.

Early childhood is here defined as birth to seven years old, the years before the "age of reason" sets in, the magical years in which we are true innocents. Young children have a pure perception of life. Unsocialized and not yet aware of diplomacy, or the art of polite lying, they tell the truth and react instinctively to every pleasure and pain.

Memories of early childhood, happy childhood that is, are perhaps the sweetest recollections of all, if only because we were so young and tender at the time.

Some people have memories of being a day old, or even of life inside the womb. But for most of us, the earliest concrete things we can recall occurred when we were around two to three years old. Think about it.

Who loved you, who took care of you?

Do you recall being picked up, caressed, rocked, sung a lullaby?

(I can distinctly remember the shape of a shadow moving back and forth across the ceiling as my mother rocked me on her lap in the middle of a dark New England winter's night. I can also hear her singing a French Canadian lullaby that called the baby a *cher trésor,* or precious treasure.)

Do you remember being dressed in a particular small child's outfit, perhaps for a portrait?

Do you remember your mother's or father's face peering at you in your cradle or crib? What was the room like in which you slept? Any brothers or sisters sharing the bedroom? What color were your pajamas or nightie? Any pictures on the wall over your bed?

What was your favorite food as a small child? Surely you remember. What about seasonal fruits and vegetables in the place you grew up (before the era of frozen foods and jet-lag produce available all months of the year), like corn on the cob in July or apples in October? And what kinds of favorite dishes did your mother (father, etc.) cook?

Did you have a pet? What was its name, what were its favorite habits, tell us about it. Did you own a cherished stuffed toy or doll to which you ascribed human personality? How about an imaginary friend?

And at what age did you go to your first school? When did you learn to read?

What was your favorite nursery rhyme or children's story or animated film? Favorite song?

Who were your playmates, and what games did you play?

How much can you remember about your childhood illnesses? Ever have the chicken pox, measles, mumps? Did you have your tonsils removed? Were you ever in the hospital and, if so, what details can you remember about the experience? My mother brought me ice cream and ginger ale in the Lawrence General Hospital after the tonsillectomy; my aunt Marie was there, too. Mothers in Massachusetts in the 1950s seemed to believe that ginger ale was medicinal; we kids got it every time we were sick. I also remember the little kid in the bed next to me had a toilet accident and soiled his sheets. Yuck . . .

And what about your parents' and siblings' illnesses or health? The illness or loss of a close family member can be a great factor in making your childhood unhappy or disturbed. Novelist Jack Kerouac never quite got over the death of his brother Gerard, who died at nine years old when Jack was four. Gerard was a real angel in his little brother's eyes, a saintly child with visions of heaven and the Blessed Virgin, spouting phrases the nuns raced to write down. Kerouac's book *Visions of Gerard,* a poignant tribute to his sickly brother, is among his best work.

Were your mother or father ever in the hospital, seriously ill, or did you lose one of your parents in childhood through divorce, abandonment, death, war, poverty, hardship? As painful as these memories may be, they are critically important to your development and your autobiography. Try to reconstruct every detail.

Did you have a lot or a little emotional security as a child? What did you fear the most? Did you worry about losing your life or your family in war or other disasters, and how did those worries affect your childhood? I can recall in the Cold War environment that we schoolchildren were drilled in air raid preparations and generally warned that World War III might be around the corner.

The dire scenario spelled out for us by grade school teachers left me and no doubt millions of other kids with horrific nightmares. Who were those evil, godless Russian Communists anyway, and why did they want to take over St. Patrick's School in Lawrence, Massachusetts?

It's been said that what happens in your first years influences your entire life. "The Child is father of the Man," as the poet Wordsworth wrote. That's why we pay psychiatrists' fees to help us remember, sort out, and analyze our earliest experiences. You may have repressed painful memories just to avoid reliving bad times, but if you want your autobiography to be honest and complete, you have to first be honest with yourself. Even pleasant memories of early childhood can sometimes have a bittersweet edge, for example when the people you loved have since died or left you.

Psychiatric therapy is not the only way to enhance your memory and "realization" of childhood. Other ways include:

- Conversations, letters, phone calls with siblings and friends you grew up with, people who shared the childhood experiences with you.
- Published accounts of life in your hometown, such as newspapers and archives dating from your childhood. The public library may prove to be a treasure trove of information. Cynthia Williams of Carmel, California, now in her seventies, was delighted to find all kinds of information in the yellowed back editions of the weekly *Carmel Pine Cone* about her father, Ted, who'd died when she was very young. In

addition, the paper had published letters
from her brother Dick written from the front
lines of World War II.

- Memory prods dating from the years of your
childhood, such as popular songs, movies,
books, fashions and styles, cultural and political artifacts may help you recall. Sometimes
just the first few bars of a song can bring back
a whole lost afternoon or summer vacation.
The taste of an old-fashioned root beer, the
TV rerun of *Gone with the Wind*, the Bazooka
comics that came wrapped around pink bub-
ble gum, or any little thing dating from your
childhood can set off an avalanche of remembering. So, write it down while it's on your
mind! Keep notebook and pencils on hand at
all times, even on your bedside table in case
you wake up from a vivid dream of youth.

- Meditation and quiet reflection. Try setting
aside some time when you can't be disturbed,
even if it means leaving your house and going
to a park or library, any kind of quiet, peaceful place where you can think back on your
childhood, visualize it, relive it.

Did you have a happy childhood? Are you happy
now? If so, chances are you were happy then, too.
The question is not whether you had it easy or
tough, rich or poor. The answer lies in love. The
honest answers strengthen and enrich your autobiography more than any others.

WHERE DID YOU GO TO SCHOOL?

Our memories of school days can remain astonishingly vivid even into old age. Certain great events can stand forever—perhaps the time a favorite teacher bestowed an honor, or the day you developed your first romantic crush on a classmate.

The "school days" in this chapter, and in your autobiography, are grade school experiences, from the ages of seven to fourteen. High school and college days are covered in the next chapter, "How Did You Come of Age?" But your earliest school experiences may have been the most formative.

Going off to school for the first time is a bit like an initiation into the rites of social conduct, following that innocent and carefree period (for many of us) in which you stayed home, safe in the nurturing environment of parents (usually the mother) and the family domicile. From that first day of school, however, your life changed forever. You were not a baby anymore. You had work to do, a daily routine, a job.

Can you remember what your very first school building looked like? (Of course you can. Who could ever forget?) Write a description of it. Was it a large, forbidding, brick structure in the city, packed with hundreds of urchins, or a quaint one-room schoolhouse in a farming community? Did it have a playground or outdoor play equipment nearby? Did you walk to school, ride a bus, or were you driven by your parents? Did your mother or father take you to school the first day? Did you cry when they left you there?

What was your very first teacher's name? Even if you can't remember her name, what did that person look like? Your entire attitude toward school, not to mention other aspects of life, may have been influenced by that first teacher. Was she a "peach" with a kind attitude toward small children, a stern man with rimless eyeglasses and a stick, a big, penguin-like nun with a booming voice?

And what about your classmates? Any particular favorites or dreaded enemies? One of our "Lit Biz" students dropped out of kindergarten solely because he was made to sit next to a neighborhood girl he detested (at age five) because she had clammy, wet hands and the class routine included a daily game of "ring around the rosy," in which he was forced to hold her hand. He simply played hooky until his mother agreed to let him drop kindergarten and start first grade a year later. "Mikey's too young to be away from home," she reasoned, little realizing the problem was only Patty Reno's palms and "a pocket full of posy." (The fun part was "Ashes, ashes, we all fall down," at which all the kids crashed to the floor.)

What do you remember about the lessons you were taught? When did you learn to read, and what was the first reading material you conquered? For several generations of children, it was the "Dick and Jane" series of readers, featuring lily-white children with a dog named Spot, who lived in an impossibly pleasant suburban home where Mom always had cookies in the oven and Dad arrived home from work in a cheerful, not abusive, mood. Or you may have learned to read from the comic strips in the daily paper, or out of sibling rivalry with an older child in the family.

When a teacher praises (or criticizes) a small child in the classroom, the effect can be devastating and far-reaching. Did someone's kind words encourage you to study and excel in school? Conversely, did an unkind or punitive school authority leave you with a bad attitude for life? Were you humiliated in front of your friends, or helped by the intervention of a teacher who saw your potential?

What was your favorite subject in school? Did that favorite subject follow you through life, helping you in your career decisions? Everyone is unique, of course: some of us pursued an early interest through a lifetime of accomplishment, while others had no interest in school and developed an occupation or passionate involvement only later in life. But if you really loved English or math or science, music or art or history, in school, chances are good that you still love that subject today!

Going to school is more than just an academic pursuit, of course. At the young age we're talking about, it's an introduction to all the arts of social adjustment, it's a way of life. How did you adjust to that new way of life? Did you spend your entire grammar school years in the same place, or move around from school to school, city to city?

Who were some of your early friends? Kids' friendships are sometimes more important to them than family relationships, and your friends were typically the kids you saw every day in school. If you grew up in a small town or school district, you may have been grouped with the same class of children for eight years in a row, a formidable affiliation rivaling even the family unit.

These early friendships may prove to be the glue of your entire social fabric later in life. They also taught you how to relate, how to share, what to expect from other people in reaction to your behavior. If I pull Susie's pigtails and make her cry, she'll turn me in to the teacher for punishment; but if I treat her nicely, she'll bring me home to her mother's kitchen for chocolate chip cookies. The Golden Rule becomes manifest in little daily transactions between children.

Can you reconstruct a typical school day routine? What time did you get up, and who woke you up— mother, father, older sibling? What did you usually have for breakfast? And what time did you leave home?

What time did classes begin? Choose a specific grade and age, and focus on reliving that period. What was the teacher like, what subjects were you studying, how were your report card marks?

When lunchtime came, did you walk home, carry a brown bag lunch, or eat in the school cafeteria or local diner/sandwich shop? Remember as well as you can the kinds of things you ate for lunch—the things you hated as well as the ones you loved.

At the end of the class day, did you participate in after-school activities, sports, Girl or Boy Scouts, etc.? Describe those activities as well. Did you wear a uniform, win a merit badge, bake brownies for the church bazaar? Or did you race home for the latest installment of a favorite radio or TV show, or to do chores for your parents?

Kids have their own peculiar ways of viewing reality. At the age of seven or eight, I used to wonder why the newspaper would print a photograph of an accident victim broadly smiling (a posed picture taken at some earlier time). "If that guy is dead, what is he smiling about?" Also, when my mother said "Rome wasn't built in a day," I thought she was saying "*Roland* wasn't built in a day." I imagined my uncle Roland being built, day by day, like a house under construction. Do you remember little misunderstandings and confusions like that, things you believed when you were very young?

Somewhere around the double digits, when you turned ten or eleven years old, a subtle but very real change happened. You became old enough to be home alone, perhaps even to take care of younger siblings, hawk newspapers in the street, shine shoes, or help your mother with cooking. Do you remember that transition from small kid to big kid, and the ensuing power that came with it?

What did it feel like? What could you do that younger kids couldn't?

Where could you go on your feet, on your bike or your horse? How did your world open up? And who did you go with, who was your best friend? Describe him or her and tell about some of the games and adventures you shared.

Did you ever do something really bad, something you would surely have been punished for doing, but got away with? 'Fess up! The little sins of childhood, which seem so huge when we're young, can be charming in retrospect. Like the time my pal Roger and I pushed an abandoned car over the waterfalls of the Merrimack River and sniggered in delight and nervousness as the horrified townsfolk called for rescue squads and fire trucks.

Did you do something so wonderful and virtuous that it gained you the applause and respect of the community? Maybe you sang a solo in the church choir, won first prize at the county fair, hit a home run in the Little League championship, or rescued your baby sister from a blaze.

Did you live in a climate where the weather occasionally forced closure of the schools? Remember the boundless joy of those "no school, all schools, all day" snowy mornings? Remember other weather-related conditions affecting your school life: galoshes in the rain; slick, thick, rubber raincoats; the wispy, tender softness of the spring and the awful boredom of longing to be outside instead of in geography class; the suffocating heat of un-air-conditioned classrooms in early summer and fall; the sweet anguish and anxiety of the World

Series game played in the afternoon of a golden, crisp October?

Did you ever play hooky?

Run away from home?

Have a pet?

Wet your pants?

Where did you go to school, and what happened to you there? How did you make the grade between seven and fourteen, between the age of reason and the onslaught of puberty? How did you learn and grow? What great lessons did you learn, if any? Who were your heroes? And what did you think you would do with your life?

For most of us, the schooling experience took a dramatic turn when we were around thirteen or fourteen years old, when we graduated from elementary and entered high school. This was a sea of change, a vast and wrenching growing up. As a little kid in grade school, you looked up to the junior high and high school kids as giant monsters, possessed of strength and size and awe-inspiring freedoms. You probably wanted to get older with impatient anticipation. (What an irony it is, now, to find ourselves older and viewed by the younger generation as dinosaurs and mastodons.)

As early schooling came to an end, you came to an age that marked the beginning of your "real," or adult life. Nearly all cultures on earth recognize this age, this transition into adolescence, with a formal ritual of initiation. Did you have one? Jews have bar and bat mitzvahs, Christians have confirmation. In some places young boys go through a first hunt or kill, while girls are removed from society after their first menstruation, to be taught the arts of womanhood. In our modern world, the traditional initiations have been largely abandoned, but we make a great deal out of school graduation ceremonies.

In any case, you grew out of early school and came of age. Before you close the chapter on where you went to school, however, spend enough time to ensure that you've described the experience fully. Especially, try to leave us with an understanding of what the schooling did to develop your basic character, talents, knowledge, and social instincts. From seven to fourteen, you emerged. You changed from a child to a budding adult. You were transformed. This period of your life deserves a major emphasis in your life story.

HOW DID YOU COME OF AGE?

Another way to phrase the question "How did you come of age?" is "How did you survive being a teenager?" This chapter, and the next chapter in your autobiography, concentrates on the ages fourteen to twenty-one, a period of life we all remember but not always fondly. Adolescence can be a trying experience whether you are hindered by poverty and misfortune or raised in a mansion and introduced at a debutante ball. Teenagers are terribly self-conscious and therefore easily embarrassed. For many, these years are best forgotten.

At the same time, however, the period in which you came of age was the most magical, intense time in your life. And your telling the story in your book puts you in the company of great literary writers from all nations. The coming-of-age novel or book is a literary genre all its own. Think of Booth Tarkington's *Seventeen,* J. D. Salinger's *Catcher in the Rye,* or, more recently, Paul Monette's nonfiction *Becoming a Man: Half a Life Story.*

Why do we call the adolescent years "coming of age"? Perhaps it's because we experience for the first time a sense of selfhood, a personal ascension to power. During this period, you became a nascent grownup yourself, entitled to opinions, able to drive a car, join the Army and fight or die in a war, and—yes—explore your emerging sexuality.

Did you do things as a teenager that were intended (consciously or otherwise) to establish yourself as an adult and leave childishness behind? Smoking cigarettes is the perfect example. The tobacco lobby knows very well that most smokers started puffing as teenagers, which is why their advertising has a juvenile tone including cartoon characters and young lovers.

What else did you do to grow up in a hurry? Forbidden lipstick, a training bra, a wrapped condom carried deep in the recesses of your wallet, protection for an event devoutly to be wished?

Sex may not have been the obsession of your teenaged existence the way it seems to be for kids nowadays, but it's a fair bet that you thought about it constantly, even if you never acted out a fully realized sexual conquest. Do you remember who told you about the birds and the bees, how you came to find out about the mysteries of your own hormonal changes and those of the opposite sex? Did you experiment with friends of either sex? Who and how was your first "real" date?

How did you view your own body? Were you vain, pleased, horrified, acutely aware of every pimple, too fat, too skinny, too short, too tall? Did you ever wish to have the body that some classmate or friend had, instead of your own? Did you adopt a fashion aesthetic, a certain hair style, a trendy look? Or, were you so serious a child that none of that mattered?

Who were your heroes, your inspiration? It's natural while coming of age to look up to a role model, and you were lucky if yours did not, in the end, disappoint you. You were in the process of forming an identity, a political ideology, a profession, a life. You looked toward some example of how to be an adult, of how to be in general. Was it a favorite teacher, one of your parents, a star athlete, an entertainer, even a politician? I was seventeen and a firm believer in Camelot when John F. Kennedy was assassinated, but by age twenty-one I was writing editorials for the *Boston University News,* calling for the impeachment of Lyndon Johnson over the Vietnam War. After Kennedy's death, my heroes were all writers: James Agee, Henry D. Thoreau, Kurt Vonnegut, Jr.

Your intellectual life begins in adolescence, too. What books did you read? What high school subjects did you like best, and what was your major in college? Try to re-create your emerging life of the mind. Do you remember the thrill of first learning some important facts of science, medicine, astronomy, art history, literature?

Youth has its privileges, one of which is passion and another foolishness, or call it naïveté or innocence. Were you passionately foolish? Did you run off and join the Navy to fight the Japanese in World War

II, or perhaps run off to Oxford or Canada to escape the draft during the Vietnam conflict? Did you fall in love, elope, get married, or have children before reaching the age of twenty-one? Did you take a chance and travel to faraway places on a freight train or cargo ship or "by thumb"?

What did you think of the Almighty? Did you embrace your parents' religion, rebel against it, or perhaps find some philosophy or spiritual belief on your own?

How did historical and social events affect your youthful coming of age? Was your life or education disrupted by war or other social calamity? Did the social events of your youth provide you with a political outlook that remained throughout your life, or did later years change your mind?

Make a list and write a few sentences about the people who influenced you in your youth. They don't have to be people you actually met in person, but the list could include your parents, favorite teachers, political leaders, writers, thinkers, singers, and musicians (some of us "come from" the Sinatra age, others from the Bob Dylan generation), religious or spiritual advisers, star athletes, or business tycoons, anyone whose life or words inspired you in your formative years and had a direct impact on decisions you made.

If you went to college, this chapter is the place to record your memories of the Alma Mater and everything that went on there. This could be a gold mine of material!

What made you choose the college you attended, if indeed you had a choice? Was it the location, the particular course of study, the fact that your father went there, the cold reality of tuition and good fortune of a scholarship? Was it just that your best friend, with whom you couldn't be parted, was going to the same place? Or that only one college accepted you? Or did you have to choose from a number of offers?

On the day you entered college, did you have a conscious plan of major study, with a career goal? Did you take liberal arts classes or some preprofessional education? And did that major and that career goal remain the same throughout college— or did you switch paths, as so many do?

If you lived at college, it may have been your first experience living away from home. What was your first dorm room or college apartment like? Re-create the experience of roommates, the excitement of being on your own.

Write about your friendships and romantic liaisons during the college years.

If you have remained in contact with college friends, invest in a few phone calls and write some letters to renew acquaintance and remember old times together. The people you "grew up with" are your best source of memory stimulation. Remember the things you did together for fun or mayhem.

How long did you stay in school, and how well do you think it prepared you for adulthood and professional responsibility, if it did that at all?

If you didn't go to college, of course, you assumed adult responsibilities earlier in life, which may have worked to your advantage if you were precocious, ambitious, or just had no choice but to plunge into full-time working and living without the benefit of an academic honeymoon.

Tell us about your high school experiences, or whatever experience you had between the ages of fourteen to twenty-one. How far did you get in school? Why did you quit, and what happened to you immediately afterward? Did you get a job, get married young, suddenly become a parent?

We learn as much or more from examples and experience as we do from books. If your great teachers were not college professors, they may have been employers, co-workers, friends, or some person who took you under his wing. Who did you learn from? Who taught you the ropes early in life, when you were testing your wings? And what ropes did you learn?

If you could live it all over again, what would you change? Do you believe the lack of a college education impaired your progress in this life? Did you find your education in doing, in the so-called school of hard knocks? Would you have spent more time in school if you could have? And what advantages do you think you gained by joining the full-time work force or family business after high school or grammar school?

In any case, you came of age in your own way. The birth of your adult personality came slowly, over a stretch of teenage and young adult years. A fully realized person emerged from the seed pod of a young child. How did you do it?

7

WHERE IS LOVE?

"Love conquers all," as the adage says, and everyone knows that love is more important than money and a close second to good health when it comes to happiness. How has your love life been?

For purposes of your chronology, love and marriage come along at this point because for most of us, love is a youthful thing, mating happens in early adulthood, children follow, and so forth. But we all know, too, that love is something you need every day of your life and even those in middle or old age can fall in love! It could happen to you—again!

The stories people write about how they found their spouse or perfect mate are among the great stories of the universe. We all recognize instinctually the importance of the attraction between lovers, a force too great to resist, the highest moment of our lives.

Even before answering questions about your great love (or loves), consider the evolution of your desire.

What did you seek, what did you think you wanted in a lover, husband, or wife when you were young and inexperienced? What did you long for?

Did you find it in the person you eventually married, or settled down with? Or did you learn some new quality of attraction when you finally met Mr./Ms. Right?

If in fact the right person came along, what was it about him or her that attracted you initially? We want the juicy details! What was she wearing on the night that you met? How were you introduced? Did you dance, dine, wine, and woo, or did you meet at a church service, neighbor-hood block party, school function, singles bar, or on the job?

You may have fallen in love, married, or otherwise created a domestic partnership more than once in your life, of course. If you have more than one story to tell, you're that much the richer.

But at this point in your story, your chronology of your life, we're looking at the first love, the young courtship, the traditional coupling that signals the end of childhood and beginning of mature love.

When did you meet your true love? What was the exact date, time, place, and circumstances?

Who else was there, if anyone? Any witnesses?

What's the first thing you said to each other, at least the first thing you can remember?

What happened on that first meeting? Dinner, a date, a conversation, just a knowing glance?

When did you realize you were getting serious about each other? Was it instantaneous, or did it follow some time later? Did one of you pursue the relationship more intently than the other, i.e., was one the chaser and the other the chased? And were you both chaste? Sorry, inquiring minds want to know!

What did you initially find most attractive about this person? What did you find unattractive, or even offensive?

How long was your courtship, and what happened during it? Try to provide as many specific details as possible. Visualize and concentrate on that period in your relationship when you were getting to know each other. Did you have any funny misunderstandings? Tell about the first time she cooked you dinner, the first time he took you dancing.

When did you meet each other's family and friends, and what was that experience like? Did her family immediately like you, dislike you, or feign neutrality? Were you turned off by his choice of buddies? Were there any problems based on different religion and social standing?

When did you pop the question, or when did you two decide you had to live together and share your lives completely?

Did he ask your parents' permission to wed?

Assuming you got married, tell us everything you can recall about the wedding and honeymoon.

What is this thing called love?

Two students write about their true loves:

"He just kept coming around until I gave in and said yes," wrote Minnie F., celebrating her fiftieth anniversary with husband Fred. They met when she was only twelve, he was fourteen. She was shepherding a flock of geese from her grandmother's field in Fresno, California. He pulled up from behind on a bicycle and made a slow turn around her in a circle. "Where you going with them geese?" he asked. "Just never you mind," she retorted. Ten years later, they were married, Minnie having had no other beau and Fred only slightly the worse for a stint in the Army. Now they live in retirement in San Diego. "I'm still his little chickadee, the top banana in his grocery," she wrote.

Robert H. remembers:

We were pen pals before we met. It was an odd way to get acquainted, certainly. We were put together by a mutual friend, Mike Y., who was Melissa's classmate at graduate school in Ithaca, New York. In order to finish her master's degree in international business, she had to serve an apprenticeship abroad, and Mike knew that I had a small mail order book business, selling U.S. titles to the French and Germans.

"Look, Melissa can go to Paris and Frankfurt and meet your clients and write a paper about the book business in Europe," Mike said. "All you need to do is sign a form rating her performance in the business. You don't have to pay her, and she'll bring good will to your business." Never mind that I'd never laid eyes on this woman, much less hire her to be my apprentice in Europe.

So she went over, and we exchanged letters for three months. Every week or so, I'd get a terrific let-

ter from this stranger, full of gossipy news about my
friends in France and Germany. They assumed she
was legitimately my ambassador, of course, but she
was embarrassed when they asked personal questions about me that she couldn't answer.

"Just who or what are you, anyway?" one of her letters asked. Some guy in Lyons, hearing that she was
my representative, had asked her if she was carrying
any hashish from the States. Just a joke, of course,
but she didn't know whether to take it seriously.

Finally, she returned to New York, I signed her
master's degree papers, and we made a date for
dinner in the Village. It was a little Greek place, a
hole in the wall really. After a couple of drinks and
lots of funny stories about my buddies in Europe,
she said, "I could make you a better dinner than
this place has. I've got my friend's apartment on
Sutton Place for the weekend. How about some real
crepes suzette?"

The rest, as they say, is history.

Given its importance, love is something you can't
say enough about, yet it can be one of the most difficult subjects to tackle in your writing. It's too
plain, you may think, to simply say that you love
someone, that you fell in love. But try to explain
the sensation, and you may find yourself tongue-
tied. At least, then, write down all the details you
can remember: the names, birthdates, family back-
grounds of all the people you loved, the way you
met, the years you spent together, the good times
and the bad. If you were separated by divorce or
death, include those details too even if they are
painful to recall.

Next to yourself, nobody is more important to
your autobiography than the person or persons to
whom you gave yourself completely.

WHAT ABOUT THE KIDS?

"Marriage and children will put the fear of God in any young man. Suddenly you're not allowed to be broke anymore!" That was one writer's assessment of the fundamental change that happens on the day your first child is born. It's as if your own life has partially ended, the energy flowing to the baby and the new life spliced out of your old one. Nature has cleverly provided that parenthood happens (usually) to young adults, people who are strong enough to withstand the blow. Having children is the greatest privilege, wonder, burden, responsibility, joy, sorrow, overall the single greatest experience many people ever have in life.

No wonder, then, that some parents allow their children's lives to dominate their own, to the extent of boring their nonparent friends to tears with incessant accounts of little Janie's and little Johnnie's cute sayings, school triumphs, even digestive habits. Later on, they subsume their life energies into concerns for the kids' college education, careers, etc., and finally into the lives of their grandchildren. "If I'd known grandchildren were so wonderful, I wouldn't have waited so long to have them," quipped one student.

If you don't have children, you can skip this
chapter just as you'd like to skip your friends'
tedious obsession with their offspring. If you do
have kids, though, you'll recognize the obsession in
yourself.

Your children and grandchildren are an essen-
tial part of your autobiography as much as they are
of your life. Their life stories become mini-biogra-
phies within your own book. They are, literally,
extensions of your own life, certainly something to
be proud of, occasionally the source of great
anguish as well. Try to be honest in writing about
your heirs, within the limits of good taste and with
a minimum of hurt feelings.

When were your children born? Give dates, places,
birth names.

When were your grandchildren born? More dates,
places, and names, and of course the names of
your sons- and daughters-in-law, or, anyway, the
people who co-parented your grandkids with your
own children. The experiences of having children
and grandchildren are different indeed, but related. The experience of your own children's birth
may have been overwhelming, something that
defined and changed your life forever, while your
grandchildren's births were a generation apart.
Sometimes, however, the grandkids move in with
Gramma and Grampa and the actual living experience is comparable.

Every child is unique. Try to explain what each of
your kids was like. Tell us an anecdote or story

from their early childhood which shows how that child developed, how his or her personality stood out. Maybe little Jeff displayed an early talent for throwing a baseball, little Sarah was a precocious musician (or perhaps it was Sarah who threw the baseball, Jeff who played the piano). What about your child or grandchild stood out in early life?

Can you trace those early influences to later developments in the children's lives? Did something you noticed early become an important part of the child's personality or life path? Explain how.

Where did your kids go to school? What subjects did they enjoy or excel in? Were they fond of school and did they get good grades, or did they hate it and play hooky? Did your kids ever gain special recognition at school, such as performing in the school play or scoring a touchdown in the big Thanksgiving game?

How long did your child live at home, if indeed your child has left home yet? If and when the kids set off on their own, how did they do it? A college apartment, a stint in the Army, an elopement, or just a gradual cutting of the apron strings?

And how did they "turn out"? This question encompasses everything from their marriages to their careers to their parenting of your grandchildren.

How often do you see your children and grandchildren today? Do they live nearby or far away? What careers and professional lives did they undertake? Do you still provide support?

Would you say you have lived your life for your children's sake in some significant ways? Decisions you made, jobs you took, sacrifices you made on their behalf? Name them and tell us the stories.

What's the proudest moment you ever had as a parent, celebrating some great accomplishment your child had?

Conversely, what's the worst thing your child ever did, the most dangerous or hurtful thing to you?

Did your kids take, refuse, or ignore your advice, generally speaking? If you could give your children some wisdom or advice today, what would it be? If you could help them overcome their problems, what would you do?

Do you find your children and grandchildren have a better standard of living than you did, about the same, or a lower one? What about their hopes and dreams and future possibilities? Is the world a safer and better place for the people you've brought into it?

Will you be able to leave your children some lasting impression of yourself, perhaps your book, heirlooms, keepsakes, an inheritance? And what is their inheritance of values, spirit, language, and culture?

What did you pass on to your children that you yourself received from your parents? This isn't limited to material things, of course. It includes beliefs

and behavior, skin pigmentation, and deeply root-
ed psychological traits. What did your parents
instill in you that you tried to pass along to the
next generation?

What was it like having children? Would you do it
again? You could hardly answer no to that question unless you've given up on your kids entirely.
But, seriously, if you had to do it again, what
would you do differently?

How did you learn to relate to your children as
adults? This is a transition many of us find difficult. My son is now nineteen and writing me mar-
velously articulate letters from his home in
Berkeley, California, which he shares with other
young students and seekers. I can't consider him a
kid anymore, but it's strange and wonderful to
consider him a grownup.

When you became a grandparent, did you go
bonkers over the baby? C'mon, you know you did.
Did you feel your children gave you enough access
to the little one, not enough, or too much? Did you
become their favorite unpaid baby-sitter? If the
grandchildren were at a distance, did you indulge
in cute baby talk over the phone? Framed photos?
A new clause in your will?

Do you ever feel any guilt over some deprivation
your child suffered, such as not having you
around enough because you were working?
Conversely, do you think you spoiled your kid
with too much attention, too easy a life? Was
there some great trauma or turning point in your

child's life which changed forever the way he or she related to you?

Will your kids take care of you in your old age? The Social Security benefit system was established to make this care unnecessary, and in fact most senior citizens in this country today are better off than their adult children in terms of financial well-being. But what about the emotional care we all need? Can you count on your kids to be there?

What kind of world do you think your grandchildren will inherit? Will it be a better or worse world than the one you yourself grew up in? And what would you do to improve it?

WHO ARE YOUR REAL FRIENDS?

My friend is not of some other race or family of men, but flesh of my flesh, bone of my bone. He is my real brother. I see his nature groping yonder so like mine. We do not live far apart. Have not the fates associated us in many ways? It says in the Vishnu Purana: "Seven paces together is sufficient for the friendship of the virtuous, but thou and I have dwelt together." Is it of no significance that we have so long partaken of the same loaf, drank at the same fountain, breathed the same air summer and winter, felt the same heat and cold; that the same fruits have been pleased to refresh us both, and we have never had a thought of different fiber the one from the other!

As surely as the sunset in my latest November shall translate me to the ethereal world, and remind me of the ruddy morning of youth; as surely as the last strain of music which falls on my decaying ear shall make age to be forgotten, or, in short, the manifold influences of nature survive during the term of our natural life, so surely my Friend shall forever be my Friend, and reflect a ray of God to me, and time shall foster and adorn and consecrate our friendship, no less than the ruins of temples. As I love

nature, as I love singing birds, and gleaming stub-
ble, and flowing rivers, and morning and evening,
and summer and winter, I love thee, my Friend.
                              —Henry D. Thoreau,
          A Week on the Concord and Merrimack Rivers

In addition to immediate family, friends provide
an enormous amount of support in life, and in
many cases a friend can be more loving and caring
than one's relatives. Friendship is a kind of family,
too, and great friendships are the stuff of poetry
and history. Think of David and Jonathan from the
Old Testament, Damon and Pythias, Thelma and
Louise, Archie and Mehitabel. The greatest wealth
of all, of course, are friends that one keeps for a
whole lifetime.

The process of making friends is the ultimate
civilizer of social relationships. It starts in earliest
childhood, even before you go to school, from the
moment you are able to reach beyond your immediate family and play with a neighborhood child.
Some people seem naturally good at it, while others are shy or constrained. By definition, however,
friendship is more valuable the longer it has survived. As the Girl Scouts of America poem goes,
"Make new friends and keep the old/One is silver,
the other is gold."

In a way, people who are glibly able to make
friends and seem to have thousands of them may
be missing out on "real" friendship. It is better to
have a single friend who will stand by you through
thick and thin than a hundred fair weather friends
who don't sincerely care for you.

Author James Leo Herlihy's great line "Don't
look for a lover; be one" could as well be applied to

friendship. The way to make a friend is to be one. The path to friendship lies in your being open, helpful, extending yourself to others. What goes around comes around. If "the only way to keep a good man down is to stay down with him" (George Bernard Shaw), then the opposite is also true. The only way to cheer up a friend is to be an "up" friend yourself.

Think back on your life history of friendship, and you may recognize a pattern. Consider, too, the friendships you've lost, friends who drifted away or parted after a quarrel, and honestly assess to what extent the parting may have been your fault.

Who was your first friend, ever? This could have been the little kid who lived next door when you were three or four years old. Whom did you play with, what games did you play, what was your little friend's name? Can you remember a funny or cute incident, even a tiff or fistfight? Did you play doctor?

When you first went to school, were you the popular type of student, easily acquiring friends, or the shy wallflower desperate for attention but unable to make friends? Friendship is uppermost in importance to children in school, who spend so many hours being forcibly socialized.

Most of us have stronger memories of the friendships we had in high school and college than in elementary school. The people you befriended at college age, seventeen to twenty-one, could well be the friends you kept for a lifetime. If you still have your high school or college yearbook, it might be fun to try to contact some of your former classmates, if only for the value to your autobiography. Their memories combined with yours could lead to some amusing or touching anecdotes in your book.

Do you have a friend today whom you've known since youth? If so, that person or persons might rate a full mini-biography within your autobiography, just as much as your children do. Focus, of course, on the times you spent together. But include everything you can remember about your friend's life—his birth, education, family, children, where he lives and what he does professionally.

Expand that mini-bio to the full number of people you consider real friends, the ones you've kept in touch with throughout your life or friends who have been particularly loyal and good to you.

Would your best friend care to contribute a guest chapter or commentary to your autobiography? Even if he or she isn't much of a writer, you could use a tape recorder and transcribe a brief entry. Ask your friend to tell a story, a memoir of something that happened between the two of you. It could be as trivial as the time you borrowed his lawn mower, as profound as the day you attended his mother's funeral.

How have your friends enriched your life? Take the time to make a serious essay on this topic. Think of all the good things your friendships have brought you: laughter, sympathy, toasts of champagne on your birthday, the security of knowing there is someone who cares for you and is always willing to listen to your tales.

And how have you enriched your friends' lives? Without boasting, consider and write down the things you like to do for your friends, the ways that you can please them.

Where do you find your friends? Are they neighbors, co-workers on the job, members of your church congregation, bridge club compatriots, political party co-activists? What interests do you share in common?

Who are your real friends? The test of real friendship is simple. A real friend is a person who can put your interests ahead of his own enough to really care what happens to you and really help you in any way possible. A real friend doesn't just boast about his own accomplishments, but sincerely asks after yours. When you fail or suffer a blow, your real friend is sympathetic, concerned, and ready to back you all the way. When you succeed or gain, that friend is happy for you, takes pleasure in your happiness. Such a friend is part and parcel of your own heart, and you in turn are happy for him, suffer with him, and in general share his life with a full gladness. Real friends are great lovers of a sort—not sexual, but spiritual mates.

And if you love your friend, why be bashful about acknowledging her in your book? Give your friend a chapter and verse, a loving description, a tumultuous prose salute. Give that person a lead role in your movie, a strong character in your book, a fitting tribute to a real, good friend.

WHAT DO YOU DO FOR A LIVING?

Work is life. That's why we say, "What do you do for a living?" in reference to someone's job or profession. And in your autobiography, you'll want to reserve plenty of space and attention for your professional existence, the people you work with, the pride you feel in a job well done.

Work is life in the sense that many of us spend as much or more time working than we do in any other aspect of living. Depending on what you do, you may have spent more time working than sleeping, on a daily basis, with only a few hours left over for family or home activities.

With so much of your life tied up in work, why not give a generous portion of your autobiography to describing it and the people who shared it with you? This question isn't limited to jobs performed outside the home. Some people's work involved raising a family and making a home, a major job indeed! And many people work as volunteers for important social causes. Work is what you *do*, what you concern yourself with, the energy you expend in your life, not just what you happen to make money at.

What is your career, or: what work do you do?

Some people have a clear and simple answer to this question, a lifetime of accomplishment in a single field, while others have changed jobs and professions a number of times. In any case, describe what field(s) of endeavor have brought you income or other work satisfaction.

How did you first get started in your work? This is a broad question that could reach into your youth, education, and apprenticeship, or just provoke a story about the winds of fate. Some of us went to medical school following a childhood of intense interest in biology, struggling for a decade to achieve a physician's practice, while others stumbled on a franchise for pizza restaurants, or invented a better thingamajig. A lot of people simply reacted to the realistic opportunities of the economy they happened to live in: a coal miner in West Virginia, a raisin farmer in Fresno, California, an insurance company worker in Hartford, Connecticut, for example. Was it some intellectual attraction that brought you to your field of endeavor, or just the good sense to take what work was available and avoid starvation?

Continuing the question above, describe how your education or apprenticeship led you into your chosen career, if indeed it did.

What was your first job in your field, and how did you get the job or get started? Were you lucky, talented, privileged, helped out by a scholarship or a family connection? How did you make your first paycheck in the field of your choice? And how much was it?

Retrace the steps through which you grew, got promoted, advanced in your profession during your lifetime. This could be a long and complicated odyssey for some of us, but the story is certainly worth telling if the work experience was worth having.

What were your proudest accomplishments in the workplace? Here, you're entitled to brag or at least take credit for the things you were able to do. If you worked long and hard to pull off some major coup in business, an important piece of scientific research, or the launching of your own business, share the secrets of your success with your reader. This chapter could turn into a real saga.

No work experience is all sweetness and light, of course. What were your greatest disappointments in work? Were there projects you failed to accomplish, deals gone bad, companies gone under? What would you do differently if you could live over some of your business decisions?

"Money doesn't talk, it swears," as the singer Bob Dylan wrote. Thinking back on how you make and made your income, do you feel that money has been kind to you, a curse, or just a necessary nuisance? Do you have enough money, enough that is to satisfy your personal wants and needs?

Who were (are) your co-workers? Do you enjoy the company of the people you work with and see every day or have business dealings with on a regular basis? Include them in your story, with anecdotes about their personalities, what kinds of transactions you share, how long you've known each other. Describe the boss who hired you, or the favorite employee you hired. How about the people you liked the least, the ones you hated to see in your workplace but were forced to put up with? You can always give these people assumed names if you like!

If you retired, how long did you work, and what kind of retirement benefits, plans, and activities do you have?

And, if you are retired, do you miss your work? And what kind of new work, personal activity, have you found to replace it?

If you were a homemaker, what skills did you develop and what work made you the proudest? Did you find the raising of your children was left primarily to you because you were more often home than your spouse? What was the hardest part of bringing up the kids?

Did you hate housework, merely tolerate it, or actually enjoy it? Were you an impeccable housekeeper or something less?

Did you like to cook? What were your specialities? Did your spouse or children have favorite foods that you made? Did you find pleasure in your own kitchen, or was food preparation just a necessary drudgery?

How did your work life change when the kids grew up and moved out (if in fact they ever did)?

If you were a young person starting out in your line of work today, what advice would benefit you the most? In what direction would you steer a young individual who wanted to break into your field? Base your answer on your own work experiences. Enjoy and celebrate all the good things your work life brought to you, the triumphs and friendships and lessons. Share your wisdom about your line of work with us, the readers of your autobiography.

DOES LIFE REALLY BEGIN AT FORTY, FIFTY, SIXTY?

"Forty is the youth of your old age, AND the old age of your youth!" as one of our memoirists noted.

Forty is a milestone from which there can be no retreat, a merciless reminder of the advance of age. Suddenly, the waistline expands, hair turns gray, all kinds of minor aches and pains and medical problems may surface, bifocal eyeglasses are in vogue, and sex is a sometime thing.

Write about your middle years, how they evolved and what changes they brought. For most of us, middle age includes losing our parents, watching our children achieve young adulthood, and reaching our peaks of professional expertise. It may also include a "mid-life crisis" of adjustment to getting older. Did you find yourself? Tell how.

In her widely read 1978 book *The Male Mid Life Crisis (Fresh Starts After 40),* the book that may have in fact popularized the term "mid-life crisis," Nancy Mayer focused on a man's reaction to middle age, wisely noting that women also age, but have more resources for dealing with the changes.

"During this turbulent period, women have an important advantage over men: they are allowed to admit their dissatisfactions without censure and seek comfort when they feel troubled, confused, or ill. By contrast . . . men are sternly prohibited from confiding their troubles, confessing fears, or seeking help," Mayer writes. The male mid-life crisis thus evolves when men who have suppressed their emotions try to deny their inevitable aging by acting young again—falling in love with a younger woman, perhaps, or suddenly quitting their job to travel or go into business for themselves. "Pain and boredom are the impetus for change," she writes.

Where were you when you turned forty? This question isn't limited to your physical location, but refers to your entire life arrangement. When you turned forty, where did you work, live, how long had you been married, what was your position in life?

Did you stop to assess your future at this mid-point in life, and if so, what plans or changes did you make to ensure a better "second half" to your life story? Perhaps you started putting aside funds for retirement for the first time, or purchased a home or switched careers. Did you get more serious about fulfilling career goals?

Did you get depressed for a time? Even for a long time? What were the negative aspects and drawbacks of turning forty, if in fact you experienced some downside reactions? These might include personal, marital, medical problems, or the painful loss of one or both of your parents. Face it, getting older is "not for sissies," as the old joke says, and definitely forces us to confront the inevitable reality that we don't live forever. When did you first think seriously about death and begin to plan goals you wanted to achieve before you die?

How did you cope with the onslaught of middle age? Did you change anything about your life in a dramatic or bold fashion? Or just continue the flow toward retirement, maintaining a career track?

Did you have a fortieth birthday party and if so, who was there and what happened? (In fact, this question goes for any memorable birthday party in your life.)

What major lessons did you learn between youth and middle age? How did those lessons affect your attitude toward life in your second half?

How was your relationship with your own parents by the time you reached middle age? How about with your children? Were you thrust into the role of taking care of an elderly parent and dependent children at the same time? Did you feel overwhelmed?

Where did you choose to live, and why? Did the arrival of middle age cause you to upgrade, change, or even revolutionize your living circumstances? Did you undertake a diet, color your hair, visit a skin specialist, revamp your wardrobe, or otherwise take bold steps to hang on to whatever youthfulness you could manage?

From an ongoing autobiography:

> I was 39 when my father died in 1985. He was only 66 himself. It scared the living daylights out of me

because while both my parents were alive, I was kind of allowed to go on being a child. Suddenly, we (my sister, two brothers and myself) recognized that we had to take care of our mother, who couldn't fend for herself without my Dad's help. We knew the funeral for my Dad was only the first, that we'd have to endure another funeral someday for my Mom. And when she dies, we'll be *next*.

That year, on New Year's Eve, I finally quit smoking cigarettes, which I'd started when only 13 years old. I turned 40 in the late winter (February) and bought my first ever U.S. Savings Bond, something my father used to do. In March and April, I went into terminal credit card oversaturation for a three week tour of France and Italy in a rented car, staying at modest country inns and eating and drinking and visiting cathedrals. It was extravagant and took years to finally pay off, but I didn't care. I was 40 and determined to live before I died, and for me going to France and Italy was a major dream.

Before I turned 41, I bought a house with a swimming pool, gained 20 pounds (probably from all the French wine and lack of cigarettes), took a new job (that I hated) with a very conservative company (in order to pay the house mortgage) and started saving for my eventual retirement to the south of France, where I plan to find a little cottage and raise vegetables, reading all the classics that I haven't had time to read while working.

12

WHAT'S BECOME OF THE WORLD?

Our lives are often seen in terms of great public events like elections, revolutions, or natural disasters which happened in our time. For example, people will say, "I was born while so and so was President of the United States," or reminisce about where they were when Pearl Harbor was bombed or John F. Kennedy was assassinated.

Look at your life from a historical and global perspective, and you just might find your own existence has paralleled an exciting, turbulent, astonishing transition in the world itself. Depending on your age, you may well have gone from the horse and buggy to the intergalactic spaceship in a single lifetime, and your own body is a repository of history, a wealth of memories.

There's some myth that grandchildren like to ask their grandparents for stories about what life was like in the old days. If you have actual grandchildren, you know this is a romantic fantasy. Children live in the vivid present. But they may very well thank you profusely later on, when they have achieved adulthood and read your memoirs. If you can describe in your writing just the everyday, common experiences that changed because of

historical, technological, political, and social evolution, you can put your own life into a much higher
and nobler framework.

When you were born what kind of government
was in power? What were the social and political
realities of the day?

What changes and transformations followed
throughout your life, leading to the nation and its
leaders that we have today? Were you at any time
in your life confronted with despotic tyrants, political or religious oppression, war, famine, or other
disaster that disrupted your family? And how did
you survive those crises?

What was the principal mode of transportation in
your youth? How did your family get the news of
the day? How and where did you get groceries and
other necessities? How did you heat your home in
the winter?

As you grew up, you became gradually aware of
political and historical realities. When did you
develop your first personal set of values or beliefs?
When did you first vote, or become actively
involved in civic matters? Who did you vote for?
Did you follow your parents' general inclinations,
or strike out in rebellious form?

Try to put yourself in a "generation"—which one
would it be? Was yours the generation created by

World War I, the Great Depression, World War II, the fifties, the sixties? What is the defining event of your generation—Pearl Harbor, the stock market crash, the war in Vietnam?

What was the single most historic, earth-shaking event you can remember happening in your lifetime? This could literally be an earth-shaking thing, like the famous 1906 San Francisco earthquake (or other natural disaster). Or it could be a presidential assassination, declaration of war, or the last time the Chicago Cubs made it to the World Series.

With all the changes you've seen in the world, which ones do you think were the most useful to humanity, which ones the most damaging? For many of us, the introduction of electricity, the telephone, and labor-saving devices like the washing machine or gas range revolutionized our lives forever. (And in some parts of the world today, these things remain elusively out of reach.) Most damaging changes might include overpopulation, pollution, disease, war, or the loss of our simple sincerities. Miss Manners would sniff that the world is a much ruder place today than it used to be.

What are your attitudes, political ideals, and aspirations for the world you live in today? This is a complex question, of course, one that may easily lead you into a lengthy reply. To answer it fully, consider the conditions of your current life. Are you more comfortable than the circumstances at your birth? Who do you vote for nowadays, and why?

Try to relate your current attitudes to the lessons you have learned from historical experience. Having looked at how the world has changed, what do you see for the future generations coming up behind you? Will they inherit a better, more peaceful, or more prosperous world?

HOW DOES IT FEEL
TO BE OLD?

Joking aside, you're only as old as you feel. But mature people have every reason to feel entitled to espouse a philosophy of life and share with others the lessons that only experience can bring. What conclusions have you drawn?

Being "old" is more than a state of mind, of course. No one could possibly put himself in that category at an age lower than required for membership in the American Association of Retired Persons, for example. But many AARP members are running around the country, having a ball, and hardly feeling old at all.

Perhaps the greatest advantage of age is the respect you get, or should get, from other people. In any civilized nation, we defer to our elders and honor our ancestors for their wisdom and contributions to society. In Japan, persons of great merit can be declared a "living national treasure" with a lifetime salary from the government. The French have an *en viager* mortgage system in which the elderly homeowner sells his real estate for a sizable down payment and monthly check, guaranteed for his lifetime, and if the buyer should miss a single payment, the deal is nullified and the old person keeps everything paid. In the United States, we typically get a Social Security check, maybe Medicare, a senior discount at Denny's, and half-price bus fare.

The respect you deserve is for having lived a long time, for having survived many things, for knowing more and caring more about people.

How are you spending your retirement? What do you like to do? Have you gone fishing with your grandson, signed up for season subscription tickets to the theater, taken a college class, done the things you didn't have time for while working or raising your family? Tell us about these retirement occupations, with full details please, and a funny story or two to illustrate your experience.

Do you have any hobbies, obsessions, things that occupy your time? What do you read? What TV shows do you follow with regularity? Which sports teams get your support? Which political party do you vote for/work for? What are your most passionate beliefs?

Do you vacation or travel much? If so, where have you gone? Give us the details of your most recent trips. Where do you plan to go or where would you like to visit? Got any photos of recent adventures and excursions? Do you prefer traveling in a tour group or independently? Have you had any travel disasters, such as getting your wallet stolen in Montreal or falling ill in Rome? Even bad luck on the road can seem adventuresome and exciting in the retelling. What are your favorite memories of places you've visited? Favorite restaurant or type of cuisine you tried? The place you'd most like to return to?

Who are your heroes today, if you still have some? Who do you admire among living leaders, entertainers, writers, thinkers, friends and family? And why?

What would you tell young people about how to live? Looking back on your life, you surely found some ways of living superior to others. Your value system is embodied in advice you might offer to a young person starting out. What to study, how to make love (in every sense) to a spouse, what indeed to look for in a mate, how to work well and prosper, how to set aside for a merry retirement?

What would you do differently? It's perfectly all right to express the negative, the unsuccessful, the painful aspects of one's life, as well as the joys and triumphs. In fact, no autobiography would be honest without some moments of grief, tragedy, error, loss, or regret. What would you change in your life if you had another chance; what would you do to prevent the misfortune that befell you?

You may know the Robert Frost poem called "The Road Not Taken," in which the poet talks about how the choice of direction at a fork in the road changed everything in his life. Reflect on the forks in the road, the choices you made. How did they change your fate? How would things have come out differently if you'd made a different choice?

What will you do next? The autobiography is never really complete while the author lives, collecting new experiences and memories. So you need to include your future plans. Where would you like to go, what would you like to experience, in the relaxed years of retirement? Rather than ending your book on a note of sealed fate and certain demise, leave us with anticipation of adventures to come.

Who was (is) your favorite person, your personal MVP? If you have more than one candidate for the person in life you most enjoyed, consider yourself lucky. The person could be your spouse, longtime companion, best friend, or child, someone with whom you spent quality time in your life.

What do you like to eat, and can you eat what you like? This is not a trivial question by any means. "You are what you eat," and the older we get the more we realize how vital the diet is to good health and well-being. Things we used to eat with impunity can now bring forth digestive turmoil, and maybe we've learned some self-discipline in the pantry over a period of years. But let's include, just because it's such an important part of your life, your culinary philosophy of what's delicious.

How much do you sleep at night, and what kind of dreams do you have? Psychology has long acknowledged the importance of dreams, but they remain mysterious and unexplainable. Those who have been gravely ill, close to death, sometimes report that they stopped dreaming and dreams returned only after their health improved. Insomnia is the curse of an active mind trapped in a tired body. Too much sleep, deep lethargy, is an enemy of health as well. In all, how well and how much you sleep is a critical factor in your life.

What are your hopes and fears? These opposites reflect your anxieties about the future. What are your greatest hopes for your children and grand-children, for the future of the planet, for humanity? And what are you most afraid of, the worst scenario you can picture up ahead?

Why did you write this book? What did you hope to accomplish? It helps to put this philosophy in writing, as you yourself may know why you wrote it but your reader may not. Writing it down may also help you understand your true motives in accomplishing this monumental work. When you get to the end of your book and look it over, you may be surprised that the work itself speaks to you as if someone else had written it, and for the first time you understand its message.

If you don't write down the events of your life, who will? If you put if off, when will you get around to it? If you're in your later years, how much time do you have to get this wonderful story written? Start writing today, and you may find it addictively engaging. Writing your autobiography can be as easy as answering these questions that define you, following the craft of the memoirists of old.

THE CRAFT OF MEMOIR

The craft of memoir is all in the business of remembering and the art of retelling what happened in real life to real people. The stories should be told directly and simply, just as they occurred and with a minimum of prose embellishment. And of course you search for the truth in these stories, although some errors of fact or matters of interpretation are bound to come in. We don't remember perfectly, but we seek to project an overall impression of how things were.

It never hurts to consult other sources to verify or amplify your own memories and impressions. Chief among these sources are living people who shared important moments in your life, family members and friends and co-workers with whom you spent your time. Their recollections and stories can only enrich your own. Also published sources, old newspapers, magazines, library research, correspondence rescued from an attic, can be invaluable sources for your book.

Write as if your life depended on it, write as if you are creating a life you want others to understand and sympathize with. You are doing no less.

If your life was worth living, your memoirs should be worth writing with care and love.

Enjoy the experience. Don't write to please an audience before you write to please yourself. Let the memoir experience enhance the experience of living itself. Love every sentence, admire every page of your book, even if it isn't up to the standards of Shakespeare and Voltaire.

Dedicate your work to someone you love or admire, and that person will in effect help you to complete the book. All books should be dedicated, so why not yours? When you think of the dedicatee, you'll be inspired to produce your best work.

Dedicate your life to your book. Make the book reflect the value of your existence, your time here among us on earth. What could be better for you than respect and dedication? What could be better for your memoirs?

The marvelous writer Annie Dillard put it this way: "Writing a book is like rearing children—willpower has very little to do with it. If you have a little baby crying in the middle of the night, and if you depend only on willpower to get you out of bed to feed the baby, that baby will starve. You do it out of love. . . . That's the same way you go to your desk."

- The title of your book may change when you've finished the manuscript. Very often, even professional writers will produce a manuscript under a "working title" and postpone the final title until the work is finished and can be assessed. An editor or close family member, someone who's read the finished manuscript, may also influence your choice of a title.

- In the end, your book will be as unique as fingerprints, as special as your life itself. Don't be afraid of this particularity. Revel in it. You never set out to match your life perfectly with that of some hero or mentor. And you should have no regrets about the way your life turned out, notwithstanding the normal degree of mistakes and misfortunes. If you want your autobiography to be readable and entertaining, be honest and sincere, not flattering or unduly moralistic. Just tell it like it was, is, and will be.
- Revise, revise. Not the circumstances of your life, but the actual prose. And not at first, but only after you have finished the rough draft of the book. The more you can revise, reconsider, edit, and tighten your prose, the more likely you can create a good book. Writing is like playing the piano, it gets better with practice.
- Take pride in what you are doing. The story of your life is the most important story in the history of the world. Answer these questions that define you, and use them to generate more questions, more answers, more stories. Don't underestimate the importance of your own experience. What could be more interesting to you? Seek to find a universal moral for humanity in your own experience, and you have joined the chorus of the bards and muses.
- Don't give up. Writing your autobiography, or any book, is a long-term project. Don't get discouraged just because you have managed only a few pages a month, or even a year. Put one page after the next, just as you would one foot after another on the long march called a life-

time, and you'll come to the end of your book, just as I've come to the end of this one. But your life will never end if you can write it down and leave it for posterity.

15

RESOURCES

In writing your memoirs, you benefit from drawing on a number of resources. This appendix talks about some of the best sources of material you can use. Don't hestitate to help your story along through the creative combination of memories, records, photographs, and so forth. Draw from any and all of these resources:

- Do You Remember When? "Remember to remember," as the novelist Henry Miller wrote. The primary resource of your autobiography is simply your own recollections of events that took place in your life. Bear in mind, however, that your memories are imperfect. Did you ever notice how three different people who attended the same event will give you three distinct versions of what happened there? That's because our memory is selective. For reasons known only to your subconscious mind, you sort out and save certain memories, while repressing others.

    Back in Chapter 1, this book talked about the importance of your psychological reality compared to your physical one. You want to remember now, while writing your autobiography, as clearly and honestly as you can, even the things that were painful to remember.

I suggested meditation, but you don't need to sign up for any formal meditation class or procedure. You simply need to find a quiet place, a way, a time, and a setting in which you can clear your mind and think back on your life. What was it like? What really transpired? Take notes! Try focusing on one part of your life at a time. On any given day, while meditating (thinking) about your life, tell yourself, "Today I'm going to think about my school days," or "my marriage," or "my job."

Visualize, visualize! The psychiatric profession advises this also, in the practice of relaxation therapy. Form a picture in your mind of the way things were. Take a visual trip in your mind through the hallways of your old elementary school. Visualize that trip you made to Europe. Run a movie in your mind, the movie of your life, one scene at a time. Put it in a mental picture, then transfer that visual image to a prose one. Re-create your life through memory and visualization.

• Share your memories with others. Next best to your own memories are those of the people you shared your life with. The finest resource you could have is a spouse or best friend with whom you enjoyed many years of experience. Other people's memories may differ from yours in some particulars, but they will help you get to the truth of the matter and you are likely to find the experience highly enjoyable!

Get on the phone and start writing letters. Get in touch with old friends, schedule reunions, have long chats, talk about old times . . . and, once again, take notes.

- Walk down memory lane. Literally. If you can afford the trip, and if the place where you grew up still exists in one form or other, go there. Revisit the scenes of your youth, preferably in the company of friends you grew up with but even alone if necessary. Go to your old hometown. Find the house you grew up in. Worship in the church where you got married. Return to the battlefields where you fought in a war. Refresh your memory through actual, physical contact with the past.

- Check genealogical records. The careful science of family records may astound you. Libraries, churches (notably the Mormons), city halls, government records may contain surprising revelations about your family history. At the very least, all births, marriages, divorces, and deaths are recorded somewhere. Try to reconstruct your family tree through genealogical research. You just might find that this search is fascinating and revealing in ways you never imagined.

- Look through old newspapers, magazines, school yearbooks, company magazines published for employees, all kinds of printed material. The local daily or weekly newspaper from the town where your parents lived or where you grew up can often prove to be worth its weight in gold. Most of the dailies kept a "morgue," a gruesome term meaning a library indexed to the names of every person who was ever mentioned in that paper. If you looked up "Mungo" in the Lawrence, Massachusetts, *Eagle Tribune* morgue, you'd find I was a scholarship-winning newsboy, editor of my college paper, and eventually a reporter for that very newspaper. And you'd find the obituaries of every other Mungo in town since 1890.

Smaller newspapers may not have kept perfect morgues, but they'll usually let you have a look through their bound, yellowed back issues in order to research your past. Offer to pay for making photocopies of old pages.

School yearbooks are wonderful sources of information, as are corporate magazines, printed histories of your community, and histories of organizations in it.

- Dear Diaries. You're very lucky if you had the forethought to keep a diary, or if you can find diaries others have kept about the people and times in your life. Few resources could be more valuable and accurate. Search the attic, ask around. Did anyone in your family happen to keep a diary, is it available, could you read it or quote from it? The simple daily revelations in a personal diary can often create a beautifully detailed portrait of what life was like in a lost era.

- Scrapbooks, clippings, and notes. These are the average person's humble effort at keeping a real archive. If you went to the trouble to make a scrapbook, chances are you never threw it away. Any and all of this material can trigger your memories and provide you with invaluable details to flesh out and strengthen your autobiography. Ask your relatives and friends if they have old scrapbooks, clippings, school report cards, children's art, any bit of nostalgia saved from the past. Look through these things at your leisure, and you may find it's more entertaining than the movies or baseball.

• Letters and postcards. Like diaries and scrapbooks, old letters are priceless resources for your autobiography. If you saved the letters and cards you received, now's the time to dig them out of the closet and go through them. It's usually fine to quote from a letter in your book, but be aware that the letter itself and its literary contents remain the property of the sender. Unless the letter is from a famous author, you probably don't need to worry about copyright problems. I have letters from John Updike, Kurt Vonnegut, Gore Vidal, Erica Jong, Jessica Mitford, and many other writers which I couldn't reproduce without their written consent. But the best letters I have are from my late father, and concern family affairs.

• Photos, slides, home movies, home videos, all kinds of visual records. Virtually everyone you know has boxes of old pictures, and these can be priceless resources in helping you piece together the events of the past. Best of all are photos that are labeled with dates and names, but a lot of people never got around to the work of documenting these images. Therefore, it's helpful if you look at old photos, slides, movies, etc., in the company of relatives and friends who can help you identify the people in them.

• Government records from city, state, and federal agencies. These are telling documents, including military records, medical histories, birth certificates, official commendations, and records of deaths. For no more than a nominal fee, most innocuous government records can be accessed. Confidential, criminal, or mental health records may be more difficult to get, but perseverance usually pays off.

- Oral records, tape recordings, even telephone answering machine messages can be fruitful resources. Did your family or friends ever send cassette tape letters in the mail? Ever make a voice recording at a major family reunion or event? These things could be a treasury of material for your book.
- Other people's memoirs. If anyone in your circle of friends or in your family wrote their memoirs, published or not, their earlier work may prove highly valuable to your own. And sometimes even the published autobiographies of famous people may relate to events in your own life. Seek out and use any memoirs or written life stories from people you knew or people who lived in your time and space.
- History in general. Published accounts of public events often trigger memories that can be included in your autobiography. The same goes for old recordings of popular songs, old movies on the "Late Late Show" (recorded on your VCR for viewing at a more convenient time), any kinds of recorded history from the periods of your life.

Use these resources wisely and well. Don't worry; if you start digging around, you'll find a vast, almost inexhaustible supply of them. It's a bit like detective work, one discovery leads to another. You may well have too much material, and be forced to edit and decide what to include in your book.

A WORD ON PRINTING YOUR BOOK

We've reached a kind of limitless Nirvana in the industry of printing in the age of computers. It's never been easier to print your autobiography in a limited edition for your family and friends, at a price almost anyone can afford.

In the old days, you'd need to type out your story, have a professional typesetter retype it into "hot type," pay a lot to have a printer impress copies in ink onto paper, and so forth. Photos were even more expensive to reproduce.

You can decide for yourself how much or little you'd like to spend on reproducing your book, but the bottom line is very simple while the upper limits are sky-high. You can simply produce one well-typed version (or pay a typist to do so), then take it to a copy shop and make photocopies for a few cents a page. These can be bound in a basic clasp or three-ring binder. Even photographs, including color, can now be decently reproduced through inexpensive photocopy techniques.

Computers and their laser jet printers now make typesetting a breeze. If you don't have a computer in your home, professional copy shops often rent the use of Apple or IBM machines, and word processing secretaries can get the job done efficiently at a fraction of what it once cost to make handsome, typeset "copy."

On the expensive end of the spectrum, anything is possible. You could decide to have your book bound in a perfect binding (glue) paperback format or sewn into "signatures" in a hard cover volume with glossy reproductions of your photographs. Be careful in negotiating these matters, however, because there is always a real danger of paying too much to an operator who takes advantage of your inexperience in the publishing business. Refer to the next chapter for the titles of some books that deal specifically with production matters. If you decide to use professional printers and bookbinders, always get competing quotes from at least three companies.

As a general rule, I advise "Lit Biz" students to stay away from "vanity press" operations that will produce and publish your book for a fee. They can be quite expensive, seldom less than five thousand dollars for a finished book, and essentially you're paying a high premium for the service of having somebody handle all the publishing details that you could arrange on your own for a lot less money. The vanity presses almost never do anything to promote your book, so you're left with a garage or spare bedroom filled with unsalable books.

Your best bet is probably to sit down and estimate how many friends, relatives, co-workers, and acquaintances are likely to want a copy of your book, and produce a number of copies more or less in line with the demand. Give yourself a generous number of extra copies, of course. It's practically guaranteed that you'll meet new people every year to whom you'll want to give a copy of your autobiography!

For that reason, save the original pages or plates and photos from which your book was copied, so you can make fresh copies as the need arises in future years.

APPENDIX

OTHER BOOKS TO HELP YOU

Barzun, Jacques. *Simple and Direct: A Rhetoric for Writers.* New York: Harper and Row, 1975.

Bruss, Elizabeth. *Autobiographical Acts.* Baltimore: Johns Hopkins University Press, 1976.

Buckley, Jerome H. *The Turning Key: Autobiography and the Subjective Impulse since 1800.* Cambridge: Harvard University Press, 1984.

Burke, Clifford. *Printing It: A Guide to Graphic Techniques for the Impecunious.* Oakland: Wingbow Press, 1974.

Chicago Manual of Style. Chicago: University of Chicago Press, 1982.

Coe, Richard N. *When the Grass Was Taller: Autobiography and the Experience of Childhood.* New Haven: Yale University Press, 1984.

Daigh, Ralph. *Maybe You Should Write a Book.* New York: Prentice-Hall, 1979.

FitzHugh, Terrick V. H. *How to Write a Family History.* Rickreall, OR: Alphabooks, 1990.

Fletcher, William. *Recording Your Family History.* Berkeley: Ten Speed Press, 1989.

Hartley, William G. *Preparing a Personal History.* Phoenix, AZ: Primer Publications, 1976.

Holt, Robert L. *How to Publish, Promote and Sell Your Own Book.* New York: St. Martin's Press, 1986.

Jordan, Lewis, ed. *New York Times Manual of Style and Usage.* New York: Times Books, 1976.

Kanin, Ruth. *Write the Story of Your Life.* New York: Hawthorn/Dutton, 1981.

Krauch, Velma. *This is Your Life Story: How to Write It.* Vacaville, CA: Encore Publications, 1988.

Leibowitz, Herbert A. *Fabricating Lives: Explorations in American Autobiography.* New York: New Directions, 1991.

McWilliams, Peter A. *Word Processing Book: A Short Course in Computer Literacy*. New York: Ballantine Books, 1983.

Pascal, Roy. *Design and Truth in Autobiography*. Cambridge: Harvard University Press, 1960.

Ross, Tom, and Marilyn Ross. *The Complete Guide to Self Publishing*. Cincinnati: Writer's Digest Books, 1989.

Simons, George F. *Keeping Your Personal Journal*. New York: Ballantine Books, 1986.

Spengemann, William. *Forms of Autobiography*. New Haven: Yale University Press, 1980.

Strunk, William, Jr., and E. B. White. *The Elements of Style*. New York: Macmillan, 1979.

Zimmerman, William. *How to Tape Instant Oral Biographies*. New York: Guarionex Press, 1982.

Zinsser, William. *On Writing Well: An Informal Guide to Nonfiction*. New York: Harper and Row, 1990.

Zinsser, William, ed. *Inventing the Truth: The Art and Craft of Memoir*. New York: Houghton Mifflin Co., 1988.